THE FORGIVENESS JOURNEY
WORKBOOK

NELLA COIRO

Acknowledgements

I WANT TO ACKNOWLEDGE AND THANK the talented women with whom I've had the pleasure to work with on both projects:

To Audrey Silverman for her outstanding editing, proofreading, and invaluable suggestions and insights.

To Ariel Hudnall for her beautiful covers and interior designs on both books, and her patience in making last-minute changes and adjustments.

I also want to thank the very talented Margo Trueblood, Voice SOVAS Voice Arts Award Winner, who just completed my audiobook for *The Forgiveness Journey: Transcend Your Hurt, Transform Your Life*.

CONTENTS

CHAPTER 1	Introduction	5
CHAPTER 2	What is Forgiveness?	9
CHAPTER 3	The Science of Forgiveness	12
CHAPTER 4	The Law of Attraction and Forgiveness	16
CHAPTER 5	Are You Addicted to Your Victim Story?	23
CHAPTER 6	Pain Killers and Emptiness Fillers	26
CHAPTER 7	Self-Forgiveness & Taming Your Inner Critic	33
CHAPTER 8	The Forgiveness Steps	45
CHAPTER 9	Forgiving Your Siblings	50
CHAPTER 10	Forgiving Your Children	58
CHAPTER 11	Forgiving Your Spouse or Life Partner	62
CHAPTER 12	Forgiving Your Parents	67
CHAPTER 13	Forgiving Chronic or Serious Illnesses	93
CHAPTER 14	Forgiving Sexual Assault and Child Abuse	100
CHAPTER 15	Communication Contamination	104
CHAPTER 16	Establishing Boundaries	110
CHAPTER 17	Releasing Toxic Relationships	113
CHAPTER 18	Mindfulness Exercises & Meditations	121
CHAPTER 19	Obstacle Busters	128
CHAPTER 20	Seeking Forgiveness from Others	132
CHAPTER 21	Bonus Chapter—Living Proactively	135
CHAPTER 22	Epilogue	139
	Did You Like *The Forgiveness Journey Workbook*?	141
APPENDIX A	Questionnaire Form	142
APPENDIX B	Bibliography	145
	About the Author	147

Copyright © 2019 Nella Coiro. All rights reserved.

No part of this publication may be reproduced, distributed, or transmitted in any form or by any means, including photocopying, recording, or other electronic or mechanical methods, without the prior written permission of the copyright owner, except in the case of brief quotations embodied in critical reviews, and certain other noncommercial uses permitted by copyright law. Under no circumstances may any part of this book be photocopied for resale.

Library of Congress Control Number: 2019912115
ISBN: 978-1-7339522-2-4 (paperback)

DISCLAIMER
This work is sold with the understanding, that neither the author, nor the publisher, is held responsible for any results accrued from the advice in this book.

Some identifying details have been changed to protect the privacy of individuals.

Sunrise Valley Publishers
Carmel, New York

Author's website: www.nellacoiro.com

FORWARD BOUND

I'm turning my back to the wind,
and waving goodbye to the should-have-beens.
Walking away from yesterday,
and breathing the air of a fresh new day.

The days too quickly fly away
when we're too glued to yesterday.
The past has weighed me down too long.
Today I'm choosing a new song.

Walking with my head held high
my eyes are forward bound.
The past is gone. I'm moving on.
It's time to spread my wings and fly!

The sun has set on yesteryear.
I'm done with shedding rusty tears.
I see my life with fresh new eyes.
I've finally bid the past goodbye.

Walking with my head held high
my heart is forward bound.
The past is gone. I'm moving on.
as I spread my wings and fly!"

Nella Coiro

I

INTRODUCTION

*If we continue dwell in the pain of the past,
we are allowing valuable—even beautiful moments escape us.*

WELCOME TO *THE FORGIVENESS JOURNEY WORKBOOK*. In this workbook, you will be able to explore your own forgiveness journey in great depth. If you have already read *The Forgiveness Journey: Transcend Your Hurt, Transform Your Life*, you can apply the topics discussed herein on a more profound level. However, if you haven't read my first book, this book can stand alone in assisting you on your forgiveness journey.

The Forgiveness Journey Workbook contains a wide array of tools, including insightful text, insights, thought-provoking focus questions, quizzes, fill-in-the-blanks, surveys, and much more, all designed to assist you in exploring and applying each topic of forgiveness to your specific life circumstances. So, let's get started!

Forgiveness is a topic that touches everyone. I'm pretty sure that if you and I were having a conversation, you would say that you have struggled to forgive someone in your life at one time or another. Maybe you haven't forgiven that person yet. Maybe you feel that you can't forgive them unless they demonstrate remorse. Whatever the reason, forgiveness isn't easy and requires work.

This raises the question: What is it about the idea of forgiveness that makes a lot of people cringe? We want and usually expect others to forgive us if we have offended them. However, when we're sitting on the opposite side of the table, and we're called upon to forgive someone who has offended us, it can be unnerving.

And, if that's the usual reaction, then why forgive at all? Especially if the offender is unapologetic. Or, maybe that person has been a thorn in your side for years.

Here's the problem: If we don't forgive and move forward, then, day after day, we carry the burden and the weight of feelings such as hurt, anger, thoughts of revenge, sadness, loss, disappointment, frustration, anxiety, and others. Eventually, these feelings will begin to dominate our lives, impact upon how we relate to others and our world, and can even cause serious emotional distress, and possibly physical illness. Moreover, if we continue to dwell in the pain of the past, we are allowing valuable, even beautiful moments to escape us. Is this how you want to spend your remaining moments, hours, days, and years?

It is impossible to maintain any level of serenity in this state of mind, and the only way to emerge from this place is to *choose* forgiveness. Yes, it *is* a choice. That doesn't mean that it's an easy one. In fact, right now, it might seem to be an impossible feat. This is why sometimes we must suffer and struggle with internal battles, before we are ready to make this choice. Until we do so, however, we are giving the offender the power to control our emotions and our valuable time. Essentially, in harboring resentments, we are allowing the offender to *own* us. I definitely don't want anyone to *own* me. Do you?

THEN AND NOW

And yet, if you told me a decade ago that I would write, not one, but *two* books about forgiveness, I would've looked at you as if you were completely insane! Especially if we were acquainted, and you knew my views and struggles concerning this issue. The word *forgiveness* was definitely not a part of my every day vocabulary. And yet, here I am, talking about the benefits of forgiving, and completing this second book.

What happened to change my mind? I looked at my life and I realized that while I was wasting time ruminating about the unchangeable past, the days and the years were passing me by. Moreover, I was failing to live them fully, because my focus was not in the present moment. I also recognized that embracing resentments came with too high a cost. I couldn't maintain any level of serenity for very long, because my life and my thoughts were overshadowed by these negative feelings.

So, one day I thought about the biggest resentment I had, which was toward my mother. Even though she had passed away many years ago, the resentment lived on, and I decided that I wanted to be rid of it. I also knew that if I could release this major resentment, then I would be able to let go of the other grudges with ease.

I thought to myself, "Where do I start?" Then, something told me that I needed to step away from my own feelings and look at what my mother's perspective might have been. With pen and paper, I started to write my mother's story. I wanted to capture a glimpse of what her life and her world might have looked like through her eyes.

The next day, I re-read what I had written, and something remarkable happened. For the first time in my life, I saw my mother as simply another person, separate from all of the expectations and disappointments that I've had toward her in the past. She was just another woman who has made some mistakes in her life, just like me. I have shared these insights and this process in greater deal in Chapter 12, here, and in my first book.

Suffice it to say that I felt this resentment melt away, and I was able to forgive her. This experience was so life-changing, that it inspired and led me to write my first book, *The Forgiveness Journey: Transcend Your Hurt, Transform Your Life,* and now, this workbook.

CHOICES AND PERSPECTIVES

In *Man's Search for Meaning*, Dr. Viktor Frankle, a Holocaust survivor, asserts that everything can be taken away from us, but *not* our freedom to choose our attitude and how we respond and conduct ourselves. He sees this choice as the last of the human freedoms. Consequently, Dr. Frankl chose to forgive the Nazis who committed horrendous crimes against him and his loved ones, when he was in concentration camps. (He is a role model for all of us!)

How was he able to forgive offenses that most of us would see as reprehensible as well as unforgivable? If we look beyond the actual offenses, we might capture a glimpse of why he saw the tremendous value in forgiving. Dr. Frankl was able to see the bigger picture—healing himself by releasing his resentments.

When I am doing a workshop or a public speaking event, often, someone will ask: "Are there any offenses that are unforgivable?" The short answer is "no." What?! Allow me to explain. I believe that our primary goal should be on self-healing. We need to focus on how forgiving will benefit *us*, by allowing us to let go of the negative feelings mentioned earlier. Therefore, if this is our intention, then the specific details of the offense become unimportant. This is the broader perspective that I believe Dr. Frankl considered when he forgave his perpetrators.

Once you have made the choice to forgive within this framework, you will be motivated to do the work, heal, and move forward. The good news is that when you shed the shackles of resentment, your life will dramatically change.

There was a point in my life when I felt that some offenses were unforgivable, especially those incurred during childhood. However, when I looked beyond the offense itself, and saw the bigger picture (my happiness and mental health), then I was able to see that forgiving would benefit *me*.

Please know that there is an exit door. You don't deserve to remain in the clutches of hurt, and you have the power and the strength to let go of any and all resentments. I want to begin our journey together by congratulating you in advance for choosing this path! You've got this!

HOW TO USE THIS WORKBOOK

All of the material in this workbook has been carefully designed to broaden your perspective, and to assist you in applying these principles to your specific circumstances. Before you continue, please reach deep into your heart. Without spending too much time on it, jot down a few of the beliefs that immediately come to mind when you think about forgiveness.

_____

_____

_____

_____

_____

_____

_____

_____

Now, imagine putting these ideas into a box, and closing the lid. You can open this box again after you complete this workbook. You might be surprised to see that your views have changed.

2

WHAT IS FORGIVENESS?

"Forgiveness is the highest form of self-love."

As mentioned in the first chapter, it's interesting to note that the word *forgiveness* can evoke negative feelings in so many people. Let's begin by looking at a brief summary of the common misconceptions surrounding forgiveness.

- Forgiveness is *not* surrender. We are not conceding defeat by forgiving someone. We are taking back our power and control of our lives.
- Forgiveness does not remove accountability.
- Forgiving doesn't mean pretending that everything is okay, and that nothing happened. It means acknowledging that something has indeed happened, and we are willing to forgive the offense for *our* wellbeing.
- Forgiveness should not be contingent upon an apology. When we expect an apology, we are giving away our power to the offender. Some people will never apologize. That's their journey and their karma.
- Forgiveness is not about making excuses, accepting the unacceptable, or condoning a person's hurtful behavior.
- Forgiveness doesn't mean forgetting. Some offenses are never completely forgotten.
- Forgiveness does not need to include a conversation with the offender.
- Forgiveness doesn't always include reconciliation. The forgiveness process takes place within our own hearts. You will need to weigh the pros and cons of continuing the relationship versus cutting it off.
- Forgiveness does not mean we should accept or tolerate abuse, disrespect and toxicity.

Okay, so beyond all of the misconceptions, what exactly *is* forgiveness?

- Ultimately, forgiveness is the highest form of self-love.
- Forgiveness is an act of self-compassion and self-respect.
- Forgiveness is a choice.
- Forgiveness is a shift in perception and perspective.
- Forgiveness empowers us and frees us from self-induced bondage.
- Forgiveness allows us to close the door on the past and move forward.
- Forgiveness focuses on the self, and not the offender.
- Forgiveness is giving up the desire for revenge.

- Forgiveness is letting go of need for an apology.
- Forgiveness is an act of self-preservation, not an act of self-sacrifice.
- Forgiveness is an an opportunity for personal growth.
- Forgiveness is a gift that we give to ourselves.
- Forgiveness is a learning opportunity.
- Forgiveness is the only way to heal our hearts.

I have spoken to numerous people to learn about their views on forgiveness, and three prevalent themes revealed themselves: The question was: "How do you know that you have forgiven someone?"

"I've stopped keeping count and obsessing about how many times this person has hurt me."

Have you ever kept a mental tally of offenses?

_____
_____

If yes, can you calculate how much time that you've spent doing this?

_____
_____

Do you feel that this was wasted time?

_____
_____

"I've stopped feeling a knot in my stomach, every time I think about that person."

Have you ever felt physical discomfort at the mere thought of someone?

_____
_____

Lower back pain? _____

Stomachaches? _____

Headaches? _____

Nausea? _____

Elevated heart rate? _____

Others?

_____
_____

"I've given up the need for revenge."

The desire to retaliate is so common. We think that revenge will make us feel better. It usually doesn't. Retaliating doesn't remove the pain that the individual has caused us, and often, it will make us feel badly about ourselves.

Have you ever retaliated in response to an offense?

_____
_____
_____
_____
_____
_____

How did it make you feel?

_____
_____
_____
_____
_____
_____

CLOSING THOUGHTS

Now that we have explored what forgive *is* and *is not*, and using this point of reference, the exercises throughout this workbook can be approached from a broadened perspective.

Please feel free to refer back to this chapter, if you need to remind yourself about the misconceptions and components of forgiveness.

3

THE SCIENCE OF FORGIVENESS

When we recall past offenses, our body reacts as if we are reliving the actual event.

According to the Mayo Clinic there are numerous benefits in forgiving. These include:

- Healthier relationships
- Improved physical and mental health
- Decreased anxiety (emotional response)
- Decreased stress (physiological changes)
- Less anger
- Lower blood pressure
- A stronger immune system
- Increased self-esteem
- More joy in life

Our physical health is profoundly influenced by our thoughts. Therefore, when we recall past offenses, our body reacts as if we are reliving the actual event, and the stress response is activated.

Think about someone who you are struggling to forgive, and bring forth a clear image of that individual in your mind. What is your first thought or feeling?

_____

_____

_____

Can you identify any physical changes in your body when you think about them?

If yes, list here.

_____

_____

Are you able to see a connection between your negative thoughts and your physical distress?

_____

_____

_____

According to Dr. Amit Sood (Professor at the Mayo Clinic), our thoughts wander between half to two-thirds of the day, and most of these random thoughts are negative. This means that our bodies are in a state of ongoing stress most of the day. Sood believes that we need to counteract these negative thoughts by focusing on gratitude, compassion, forgiveness, acceptance, purpose, and letting go of negative feelings.

GRATITUDE

There's an old saying, "happiness is not having what you want, but wanting what you have." Essentially, this is what gratitude is all about.

What are you grateful for?

_____	_____
_____	_____
_____	_____
_____	_____

COMPASSION

Compassion is being able to empathize with someone else, and trying to offer them comfort. It's what makes us truly human.

Write down one or more situations where you have offered compassion or support to someone in need.

_____

_____

_____

_____

_____

_____

Jot down one or more situations where you were compassionate with yourself.

_____

_____

_____

ACCEPTANCE

The serenity prayer eloquently explains the components of *acceptance*: "God, grant me the serenity to accept what I cannot change, the courage to change what I can, and the wisdom to know the difference."

In acceptance, we're at peace when a situation or a person is different from what we expected. If we could change the situation for the better, hopefully, we will try to do so. However, we need to recognize that we only have control over our own attitude and responses, and are powerless over some situations, or the behavior of others.

Acceptance is not submission, surrender, or accepting abuse or toxicity. Rather, it's looking at a situation pragmatically, doing what we can, and, if we're unable to alter the outcome, we need to let go, and move on, with grace and finesse.

Share an instance where you were able to accept a situation that you were unable to change.

_____

_____

_____

How long did it take you to do so? _____

What steps did you take to reach a place of acceptance?

_____

_____

_____

Were you able to feel relief after doing so? _____

PURPOSE

Jot down one action that you could take today that would give your life more meaning.

_____

LETTING GO OF RESENTMENTS

Essentially, releasing a resentment is forgiveness, and it's accompanied by tremendous freedom and relief.

Recall a time in the past where you were able to forgive someone and absolve yourself of your resentment towards them. Jot down any feelings that you can remember after doing so.

_____

_____

_____

ADDITIONAL RESEARCH

Here are some other research findings that cite the connection between chronic resentment and physical illnesses.

- Repressed anger can contribute to cancer.
- Anger makes the body release the stress hormone, cortisol. This can create blood sugar imbalances, suppressed thyroid function, and a decrease in bone density.
- Chronic anger increases susceptibility to colds, arthritis, respiratory problems, and asthma attacks.
- Our emotions affect brain function and blood flow patterns.
- Chronic stress can compromise memory.

Have you ever become physically ill during periods of elevated stress? _____.

Can you recall any of your illnesses that might have been related to unresolved grudges, anxiety, or stress? These illnesses could be physical or emotional.

_____

_____

CLOSING THOUGHTS

As you can see, our negative emotions have the power to create or worsen physical and emotional illnesses. The studies have shown that many illnesses can be improved or healed when we let go of our grudges, our hurt, and our anger. Forgiving can help treat the symptoms of anxiety, hypertension, depression, insomnia, asthma attacks and influenza.

(Please refer to *The Forgiveness Journey: Transcend Your Hurt, Transform Your Life,* for further details on these and other research studies.)

4

THE LAW OF ATTRACTION AND FORGIVENESS

Life is a patient boomerang.

According to the Law of Attraction, each of us is a human magnet. We attract situations into our lives based upon our beliefs, thoughts, words, and actions. Moreover, we receive the same energy we put out into the world. If we focus on negative thoughts, we will attract negative situations that share this same low frequency energy.

Can you recall a time in your life where one of your fears became a reality? _____.
If yes, share below.

_____

_____

_____

Marianne Williamson, renowned author and spiritual teacher, believes that our greatest fear isn't about inadequacy. Rather, we are really terrified by the possibility that our power and potential might exceed our expectations. We are more afraid of success than failure. Interesting, isn't it? Perhaps this is because success includes bigger challenges, more responsibility, lifestyle changes, and uncertainties.

Consider the possibility that you have the power to create your reality. What would you create?

_____

_____

_____

Write down the ways in which your life could change, if you acted upon this belief.

_____

How do you define success?

What would success look like in your life?

Imagine that all of your hopes, dreams, and goals began to materialize. How does this feel?

THE ENERGY OF RESENTMENT

When we have a resentment, we feel a lot of negative emotions, including hurt, anger, sadness, anxiety, frustration, disappointment, and possibly vengeful. These thoughts and feelings carry negative energy, and this low frequency energy will usually attract negative circumstances.

When you feel resentful, what emotions and physical sensations can you identify?

THE SEVEN LAWS OF ATTRACTION

1. The Law of Manifestation

According to this law, our mind is a powerful manifestation tool, and if we increase our positive thoughts, we will attract positive outcomes. Likewise, our negative thoughts will bring negative situations into our world. Our conscious thoughts are a choice, and we can learn how to control and change them. We *choose* to focus our awareness in the present moment. We *choose* to prioritize what we consider to be important. Therefore, our self-monitoring questions should include these:

- What am I focusing my consciousness upon at this moment?
- What can these thoughts create for me?

Are you currently mulling over any unresolved grudges? _____. If yes, jot down three negative feelings that you can identify associated with the resentment.

_____
_____
_____

Do you presently have any negative situations or events in your life? _____. If yes, list them:

_____
_____
_____

2. The Law of Magnetism

The Law of Magnetism maintains that the energy we sent out will return to us. This law is similar to the law of karma, which asserts that we reap what we sow. We will inevitably attract the energy that we emit.

Can you think of a specific situation where your negative thoughts might have attracted a negative circumstance or event into your life? _____. If yes, describe it below:

_____
_____
_____

3. The Law of Unwavering Desire

This law states that if we want to attract positive circumstances into our lives, we need to focus upon achieving our goals, while maintaining a positive attitude. In other words, *act as if*. When we are driven by pure intention, we can be fairly confident that the outcome will be positive.

These are the components of pure intention:

- Identifying and respecting your desire or goal.
- Focusing on the good feelings connected with this desire.
- Believing that it *will* become a reality.
- Acknowledging that this desire might emerge from unlikely sources.
- Recognizing that you absolutely deserve to achieve this goal.
- Taking the necessary steps to achieve this goal.

Write down a situation where you *acted as if*, and experienced positive results.

_____

_____

_____

4. The Law of Delicate Balance

The Law of Delicate Balance asserts that we need to achieve balance in our lives.

We can do so by working toward our future goals, yet still enjoying and being grateful for what we have now. If we become impatient or desperate to get what we want, *exactly when we want it*, this desperation will attract negative energy and repel positive outcomes.

Have you ever noticed that when you desperately cling to a situation, you can feel the energy of resistance, but as soon as you let go and focus your attention elsewhere, then somehow this goal is recognized and fulfilled? _____. If you've answered yes, can you share one example?

_____

_____

_____

5. The Law of Harmony

The Universe always works in perfect balance. By emitting positive energy, we will attract positive energy. When we send out negative energy, however, we will attract negative energy, and create a negative ripple effect.

Negative feelings like jealousy, fear, anger and resentment entrap us in a prison of disharmony and block the flow of positive energy. Life is so much simpler when we align ourselves with the flow of positive energy, relax, and assume the position of the calm within the storm.

Can you identify situations where you have fought against circumstances in your life, even though you knew that you could not change a thing? _____. If yes, write down these instances and their outcomes.

_____

_____

_____

6. The Law of Right Action

Life is a patient boomerang. Each day we are given an opportunity to attract either positive or negative energy. Like the Law of Magnetism, this law also states that we will eventually reap what we sow.

If we treat people badly, we will attract negative circumstances in return. These can be completely unrelated to the people we may have harmed. If we treat others with kindness and respect, then positive outcomes will come our way. When interacting with people, we need to ask ourselves these questions:

- "Is my behavior acting in the best interest of the other individual?"
- "Am I behaving with honor and kindness?"
- "How would I feel if the situation was reversed?"

Can you identify a situation where your positive thoughts or behavior resulted in a positive outcome?

_____

_____

_____

_____

Can you identify a situation where your negative thoughts or behavior resulted in a negative outcome?

_____

_____

_____

_____

7. The Law of Universal Influence

Like the ripple effect, either directly or indirectly, our energy influences everyone around us. Quantum physics is fairly new, and science is only beginning to touch the surface of the enormous and far-reaching impact that one small action can have.

Share one way that you can positively influence someone in your life today.

_____

_____

THE LAWS OF ATTRACTION, RESENTMENTS, AND FORGIVENESS

Here are some interesting questions to ponder:

- Can we experience positive feelings like serenity or happiness, when we simultaneously harbor the negative energy of resentments?
- If we love one person, yet harbor a grudge toward another, does that influence the loving energy that we feel toward the first person?
- Can the negative energy that we feel toward one person cancel out the positive energy that we feel toward another?
- How much does our negative energy influence our positive energy?

Before you answer these questions, consider the fact that withholding love is a powerful manipulation of energy. Think about a time when you have lost someone you loved. This might be through abandonment, rejection, or even death. Can you identify feelings that you may have experienced when this happened to you? If yes, share these thoughts and feelings below.

_____

_____

_____

Studies have proven that when we have negative feelings toward someone, it harms our health. Moreover, when we harbor negative feelings, our hearts and our bodies cannot shake off the residual negative energy. Therefore, our resentments can make us feel horrible.

CLOSING THOUGHTS

The Buddha said, "We are shaped by our thoughts; we become what we think. When the mind is pure, joy follows." This is the core principle of the Law of Attraction. If we choose to live with kindness and forgiveness in our hearts, and direct this energy toward those around us, that positive energy will spread to all our circles of influence.

Even if we are presented with challenges in life, we will be better able to handle them with grace and strength. It is nearly impossible to feel peaceful and joyful when we are inundated with negative feelings. I surely could not do so when I was in the clutches of the negative feelings associated with resentments. As we work through the steps of forgiveness and release our resentments and victim stories, our energy will change and bring about positive shifts in our lives. The negative energy will melt away, while the positive energy will flourish.

5

ARE YOU ADDICTED TO YOUR VICTIM STORY?

Sometimes a person can become so accustomed to living with emotional pain they don't know how to live without it.

DO YOU FIND YOURSELF obsessing about a particular grudge? _____

Do you blame the offender for any negative circumstances in your life? _____

Do you tell others about this offense to gain allies or seek validation? _____

Do you define yourself primarily in terms of your victim story? _____

Do you spend a great deal of time focusing on the pain that you associate with the grudge? _____

Do you get upset if someone suggests that you should let go of the past? _____

Do you get angry if someone suggests that *you* might be wrong? _____

Do you compare your story to others, and believe that your pain is worse? _____

Is it difficult for you to focus on the positive aspects of your life? _____

Have you shared your story with the same person more than once? _____

Do you re-live the offense in your mind several times during the day? _____

Do you find yourself rehearsing what you would like to say to the offender? _____

Have the details of your story changed over time? _____

Have you unsuccessfully attempted to stop thinking about your victim story? _____

If you have answered *yes* to most of these questions, then you are probably addicted to your victim story. You might wonder why someone would purposely choose to remain in this state.

In my work as a counselor and a life coach, I have learned that some individuals gradually become accustomed to living in a state of turmoil and pain because there is an indirect payoff—euphoria.

When we have anxiety or we feel emotionally upset, our body reacts by producing the stress hormone called cortisol, which causes us to feel "high" (a sense of euphoria), and our energy level increases. This is because cortisol activates our fight-or-flight response.

However, continual release of this hormone changes the euphoria, as it morphs into a feeling of depression. This feeling is similar to the mood crash we might experience if we drink a lot of coffee or take a stimulant drug.

There's also an emotional component that causes some people to cling to their victim stories. Sometimes a person can become so accustomed to living with emotional pain that they don't know how to live without it. When they resolve their source of pain, they feel empty. Since this feeling can be unsettling, they might inadvertently create disruption to fill this uncomfortable void. Dissolving and re-creating pain can become an endless, vicious cycle.

In addition, the victim role attracts attention from others, and sometimes it doesn't matter if the attention is negative. This behavior shares the same components of an addiction, and will ultimately leave the person in a state of frustration and unhappiness.

VICTIMIZATION VERSUS VICTIMHOOD

Victimization refers to a specific event where someone has harmed us either verbally or physically. Victimhood, however, is an ongoing state-of-mind which greatly influences how we approach every situation in our lives. If we remain in a state of victimhood for a prolonged period of time, being a victim can become our identity.

The journey from victimization to victimhood usually evolves in this way:

1. Someone has hurt and offended us.
2. We can't bring ourselves to confront this individual directly.
3. Since we are unable forgive this person, we develop a resentment.
4. We can't let go of our hurt, so we continue to obsess about the offense.
5. This chronic anger compromises our emotional and physical health.
6. Gradually, we become unable to see ourselves as anything but victims, and we relate to everyone and every situation as such.

Have you ever been so hurt by an offense that you couldn't stop thinking about it? _____

Have you repeatedly shared you victim story? _____

Do you remember the reactions of your listeners? _____

If yes, what were they?

_____

_____

_____

Did the reactions of your listeners change over time? _____. If yes, in what ways?

_____

_____

_____

Have you ever been acquainted with someone who continually shared their victim stories? _____

How did this feel? Share your thoughts.

_____

_____

_____

_____

_____

_____

_____

CLOSING THOUGHTS

No one should want to remain in the victim role forever. It's unhealthy, stressful, exhausting, and uncomfortable. Even the periodic cortisol *highs* will become irritating after a while. If we continue down this path, time will pass us by, as we waste the hours re-living past offenses. More importantly, all of our relationships will suffer, and others will begin to avoid us, because they will become tired of hearing our repetitive victim stories.

As we take charge of our lives and let go of our resentments, we will be able to emerge from the prison of our victimhood state. Gradually, we will begin to replace our worn-out stories with new and healthier conversations, and live our lives unencumbered.

6

PAIN KILLERS OR EMPTINESS FILLERS

Temporary states of euphoria won't solve the pain of resentments.

WE LIVE IN A WORLD WHICH EMBRACES THE NOTION that we can use outside solutions to fix the discomfort, flaws or pain within us. The most successful marketing strategies focus on what we lack. They attempt to convince us that products will fill that void.

If we obsessively dwell upon our resentments, we will be in a chronic state of distress. Since we will want to escape this discomfort, we might search for a substance or a behavior to numb our pain. However, eventually we are going to feel disappointed, as we face the reality that we can't escape or eliminate our pain through outside diversions.

There is an endless list of substances or behaviors that can be used to numb our pain. The most popular ones are food, alcohol, and drugs. Behavioral escape mechanisms might include compulsive shopping, gambling, and diversions like assuming the victim role, entering codependent relationships, and creating what I call "trauma drama."

FOOD

There are particular foods that can alter and elevate our moods, and create a feeling of euphoria. Cheese, sugar, and chocolate are examples euphoria-producing *comfort* foods.

Have you ever used food to escape from uncomfortable feelings? _____

If yes, give examples:

_____
_____
_____

Were there any negative consequences? If yes, list:

_____

_____

_____

ALCOHOL

Since alcohol is easily accessible, socially acceptable, and fairly inexpensive, it is a popular substance that people often use to escape. The problems associated with alcohol abuse and alcoholism are numerous and beyond the scope of this book. Suffice it to say that it doesn't numb pain for very long. If you have an alcohol addiction, I urge you to get help, join a recovery group, or go to a rehab.

Have you ever used alcohol to escape from uncomfortable feelings? _____

If yes, give examples:

_____

_____

_____

Were there any negative consequences? If yes, list:

_____

_____

_____

DRUGS

Drug addiction is now a global epidemic, and modern technology hasn't helped. The internet has created easier access to drugs, and many networking opportunities that didn't exist before. There is also increased desensitization to the dangers of buying these substances from criminals.

If you think that you have a drug addiction, I urge you to join a recovery group, go to a rehab, or seek counseling. No one escapes active drug addiction alive. However, it is possible to get clean and participate in a recovery program.

Have you ever used prescription or illegal drugs to escape from uncomfortable feelings? _____

If yes, which ones?

_____

Were there any negative consequences? If yes, list:

OBSESSIVE-COMPULSIVE BEHAVIORS

Compulsive Gambling

Compulsive gambling creates a temporary high, but will eventually cause financial and relationship problems. These issues lead to overwhelming burdens and stress on entire families, and can break up relationships.

Have you ever used gambling to escape from uncomfortable feelings? _____

If yes, give examples:

Were there any negative consequences? If yes, list:

Compulsive Buying

Those with a shopping compulsion purchase items because the act of *buying* gives the person a feeling of excitement and euphoria. Often, these individuals will return the purchased items.

Have you ever used compulsive buying to escape from uncomfortable feelings? _____

If yes, give examples:

Were there any negative consequences? If yes, describe:

Codependency

A codependent relationship happens when an individual has weak boundaries and is overly dependent upon another person. Sometimes they cannot separate their feelings from the other person's, and often they have a strong need for approval.

Since these individuals are overly focused on their partners, this diversion can help them avoid their negative feelings.

Have you ever engaged in a codependent relationship to escape from uncomfortable feelings? _____

If yes, give examples:

Were there any negative consequences? If yes, describe:

An Obsession with the Past

Sometimes obsessive thoughts can also be used as a distraction. If we obsess upon our unresolved issues, this can help us avoid our current issues.

Have you ever obsessed over childhood or other past issues and resentments, to escape from current uncomfortable feelings? _____

If yes, give examples:

_____
_____
_____

An Obsession with our Victim Stories

Like the obsession with past memories, if we cling to our victim stories, they, too, can become *pain killers*, because they prevent us from addressing and resolving our grudges.

Do you ever cling to or obsess over your victim story as a way to escape from uncomfortable feelings? _____

If yes, give examples:

_____
_____
_____

Were there any negative consequences? If yes, list:

_____
_____
_____

Trauma Drama

Trauma Drama is when an individual creates unnecessary drama or disruption.

This allows them to divert their attention, escape their uncomfortable feelings, and avoid facing difficult issues. There is a physical payoff as well. The elevated endorphin levels, adrenaline rush, and the activated fight-or-flight response emulate feelings of euphoria. In the "Big Book" of Alcoholics Anonymous, there is a passage that compares active alcoholics with tornadoes, contending that they storm through the lives of others, attempting to destroy everything in their path. This is also the perfect description of those who create trauma drama. These individuals experience ongoing excitement by launching one crisis after another, and they become addicted to this feeling, and do not consider the damage and pain they are causing others.

Have you ever been either a victim or a creator of trauma drama? If yes, explain.

_____

_____

_____

The Repetition Compulsion & Trauma Drama

In addition to the addictive component of creating chaos, there is a compulsive factor as well. Often, trauma drama addicts have grown up in dysfunctional families where trauma drama and disruption were the norm, and they unconsciously repeat these unhealthy patterns. This is called a repetition compulsion. As mentioned in previous chapters, there is comfort in the familiar, even when the familiar is unpleasant.

Now, before we point the finger at every drama addict that we have ever known, let's take an honest look at ourselves. (Surprise!)

Have you ever spread rumors about someone because you were angry with that person? _____.

Did you secretly hope that the gossip would get back to that individual and upset them? _____.

When we are angry, usually our first impulse is to retaliate. We want to upset the person who hurt us. Since most of us struggle with confrontation, we might retaliate indirectly through gossip. Then we hope that this gossip will get back to the person. It might take time, but gossip often finds its way back to the target.

This is a mild form of trauma drama. We are creating disruption and involving a third party to achieve a desired goal. It is our hope that this third party will repeat the gossip to others until it reaches the person who offended us. Somehow we think that this will ease or erase our pain. (It won't.)

Have you ever used drama or created unnecessary disruption in order to escape from your uncomfortable feelings? _____

If yes, give examples:

_____

_____

_____

Were there any negative consequences? If yes, describe:

_____

_____

_____

CLOSING THOUGHTS

Temporary states of euphoria won't solve the pain of resentments. We can't escape from the discomfort associated with our unresolved grudges for long. As the temporary euphoria ebbs, the resentment and the hurt return. The solution is to transcend our resentments by working through the forgiveness process. This will help to permanently release the grudges that contributed to addictive and compulsive behavior in the first place. As mentioned earlier, if you feel that you have an issue with addictive or compulsive behaviors, please seek counseling or a recovery group.

7

SELF-FORGIVENESS & TAMING YOUR INNER CRITIC

*Our self-talk profoundly influences
our emotions and our physical well-being.*

MOST OF THE TIME, WE ARE OUR WORST CRITICS. We judge ourselves harshly, yet our positive qualities go unnoticed.

What if… we decided to stop doing this?

What if… we vowed to do everything in our power to control that sneaky little gremlin in our mind that ignites our fears, and stops us from forging forward and fulfilling our goals and dreams?

Simply put… the barriers that stop us from growing would dissolve, and everything would change!

Do you recognize your own inner voice when it taps on your shoulder? _____

If so, do you believe what it's telling you? _____

If so, let's get to work on changing this.

We all have a critical inner voice that points out our weaknesses, tries to frighten us, and prevents us from taking risks. (This is different from our conscience, which helps us to differentiate right from wrong.) This inner voice accentuates our negative qualities and refuses to encourage us, or to give us credit for our accomplishments. Moreover, it prevents us from forgiving ourselves, because we are continually reminded of our mistakes and our character flaws. Your inner critic is throwing darts, and you're the dartboard. Now, try to imagine this conversation between yourself and your inner critic:

You: "I'm feeling pretty good. My medical issues are giving me a break today."

Your Inner Critic: "No. You really don't feel well. Your medical situation is making you feel sluggish. You look pale. Maybe you should take a nap."

You: "Really?" (You glance in the mirror, and begin to second-guess yourself.) "Actually, I think that I do look pale. Suddenly I'm feeling tired. Maybe I need a nap."

Bingo! Your inner voice has successfully convinced you that you aren't feeling well, and now you're experiencing physical and emotional changes that are consistent with this negative message. This scenario happens often, even when we're not consciously aware of it. Human beings have about 2,500-3,300 thoughts per hour, with an average total of 50,000 to 80,000 thoughts per day. Think that's mind boggling? Here's the clincher: Approximately 70-80% of our thoughts are negative! This means that we criticize ourselves (and possibly others) with approximately 40,000 to 64,000 negative thoughts every day. Whew!

THOUGHT PATTERNS LOG

The first step in taming our inner critical voice is to monitor our thoughts. We can't change what we don't acknowledge. The following exercise will take seven days to complete. For one week, jot down any self-critical thoughts that you can identify. Notice recurring themes. This process will help you to identify your thoughts, patterns, triggers and mood changes.

Here's a sample template:

Date: _____

What event/situation preceded the negative thought?

_____
_____
_____

What was your mood like before this occurred?

_____
_____
_____

Describe your negative thought.

_____
_____
_____

What was your mood like prior to this negative thought?

_____

_____

_____

Negative Self-Talk Scripts

These are some of the typical comments we tell ourselves. They have the power to alter our moods, amplify our fears and insecurities, and limit our choices.

Check off sentences that resonate with you.

____ I shouldn't have done this.

____ I should have done that.

____ I never do anything right.

____ I'm a failure.

____ I will never succeed.

____ I can't…

____ I'm doomed to fail.

____ I'll never be…

____ I don't deserve…

____ Life isn't fair.

____ I have bad luck.

____ I'm too old.

____ I'm not good enough.

____ I'm not attractive enough.

____ I'm not smart enough.

____ I have nothing to offer.

____ I'll only be rejected.

____ I'm too afraid to…

____ Why me?

____ I don't deserve…

Can you think of any others?

_____
_____
_____

We are born with blank slates. As we grow up, we are indoctrinated, socialized, and influenced by everything and everyone around us. This begins when we are babies, and we are taught acceptable vs. unacceptable behavior, with words like "no", "don't", and "stop it." Many of these learned behaviors focus on the negative. We learn from what we are told *not* to do, and there isn't enough emphasis on the positive. In fact, advertisers are notorious for emphasizing what we lack and what we need. We also learn appropriate behavior specific to our gender, age, and social class.

Some of these influences include (but are not limited to):

- Our parents and our extended families
- Our cultural background
- Regional traditions
- Teachers and other authority figures
- Religion
- Advertisements
- Social media
- The internet
- Video games
- Television
- Radio
- Music

Can you think of any others?

_____
_____

Choose three influencers and share how they have powerfully influenced your life.

_____

_____

_____

THOUGHTS AND MORE THOUGHTS

Since studies have shown that most of our thoughts are negative, this is consistent with the fact that most of our environmental influences are framed from a negative perspective. Our task is to re-program our minds, as this will help us with our self-esteem and self-forgiveness. We need to learn how to stop beating ourselves up.

THOUGHT BUSTERS

A *thought buster* is a technique that will help you to become aware of and change your thoughts. When you recognize a negative thought, use these words: *"Stop! Delete thought. Move on."* This exercise will abruptly freeze your thought pattern, redirect your thinking, and help you to take charge of your thoughts.

After doing this exercise, share an instance when you successfully used the *thought buster* to interrupt your thoughts.

_____

_____

_____

GUILT AND SHAME

Guilt is when we feel badly about a specific incident. Shame, however, is an all-encompassing feeling that makes us feel badly about who we are as people. Self-forgiveness is the most powerful step you can take to rid yourself of guilt and shame.

Guilt and shame cause:

- Self-criticism and self-blame
- Low self-esteem
- Self-neglect
- Self-destructive behavior
- Anger
- Sadness
- Anxiety

Share one situation where you behaved inappropriately, and it still haunts you.

_____
_____
_____

Do you have upsetting memories or recurring dreams concerning this situation? _____

If yes, describe:

_____
_____
_____

What was happening in your life when this occurred?

_____
_____
_____

What were you thinking about before the situation occurred?

_____
_____
_____

What was going on around you?

_____
_____
_____

Can you recall something that might have triggered your behavior?

_____
_____
_____

What were the consequences at that time?

_____
_____
_____

Are there current ongoing consequences because of this? _____

If yes, describe:

_____
_____
_____

When you reflect upon these answers, you might see a pattern where similar circumstances could trigger a recurrence of this behavior. Now, look in the mirror and tell yourself that you've just learned a life lesson. This will help you to grow as a person, and to avoid repeating this mistake again.

FALSE GUILT

If you grew up in an unhealthy family, you might have assumed responsibility for the dysfunction and stress within the family unit. If a child feels unsafe or insecure, they may try to take on the responsibility of the parents. When they are unable to live up to these impossible expectations, they may feel powerless and guilty.

If applicable, reflect upon any childhood guilt you may have, and, if you can, jot down three situations you were not responsible for as a child.

1. _____
2. _____
3. _____

Now, in adulthood, you might still experience false guilt. Jot down three situations where you might experience it.

1. _____
2. _____
3. _____

LEARNING LESSONS

Mistakes are just life lessons. Every *mistake* is a potential learning opportunity, and can teach us something new. At the very least, it may teach us what to avoid the next time. The most powerful life lessons I have learned were from my mistakes.

Can you share any examples of lessons you have learned from your mistakes?

_____

_____

_____

_____

_____

BE KIND TO YOURSELF

Sometimes we need to view our indiscretions from a broader lens. It is important to take into consideration what was happening in our lives at the time. I strongly believe that all of us did the best we could with the knowledge and resources available to us that moment. Life forces us to learn from experiences, usually in hindsight. Behavior that we thought was acceptable when we were younger, will seem immature when we are older. Have you ever looked back at a particular behavior and thought, "What on earth was I thinking?" If you can ask yourself this question, then you have grown, changed, and become wiser through experience. However, there might be some lingering obstacles that you're still unaware of. Your answers to the following questions will help you to identify possible triggers that you might still have.

Write down a situation where you behaved poorly:

_____

_____

What do you think caused you to behave that way?

_____

_____

What was going on in your life at that time?

_____

_____

Can you identify any of your thoughts that preceded the event?
_____
_____

Can you recall what was happening around you?
_____
_____

Were you reacting to a previous event that triggered this situation?
_____
_____

Can you recall your mood or state of mind?
_____
_____

Can you identify particular stresses?
_____
_____

What were the negative consequences or repercussions that it caused?
_____
_____

Can you identify any learning lessons from the incident?
_____
_____
_____

Can you cite any insights that you've learned in hindsight?
_____
_____
_____

SELF-EVALUATION: THE PERSON IN THE MIRROR

It can be easy to identify our weaknesses, but most of us struggle with recognizing our positive qualities. Along with the *thought busting technique,* the answers to these questions will give you further insight into yourself.

List three qualities that you like about yourself.

What are your strengths?

What are your weaknesses?

What lessons have you learned from your weaknesses?

Ask a friend or a family member to share one or two qualities that they like about you.

LEARNING OPPORTUNITIES

Okay, so you have made some mistakes. We all have. Welcome to the club. You might have treated someone poorly. Perhaps your indiscretion was a horrendous lapse in judgement. If you have severely harmed someone, then you should consider making amends and possible restitution. These amends can be direct or indirect, depending upon the circumstances. In the Chapter "Seeking Forgiveness from Others", we will explore this in further detail. *Every mistake is accompanied by a learning opportunity.* I have always learned more from my mistakes than from my accomplishments. In fact, many of my achievements were the result of the wisdom incurred through life lessons brought on by my own errors. We learn valuable lessons from our inappropriate words or actions. Have you ever opened your mouth before you mind has a chance to censor your words? Then, you thought to yourself, "Oops", or similar, stronger words? You've probably wished that you could go back in time and change the consequences. But since you don't have a time machine, you ruminate about the event and beat yourself up. Make a commitment to stop doing this to yourself, beginning now.

Write down three mistakes you've made and what you have learned from each of them.

1. _____
   _____
2. _____
   _____
3. _____
   _____

Keep in mind that we can learn far more from one mishap than from several successes. When we behave poorly, there are usually consequences. These consequences are part of the learning lesson. Often, when faced with the painful memories associated with our indiscretions, we want to hide or divert our attention. This keeps us stuck; we can't hide from ourselves.

CLOSING THOUGHTS

When we continue to berate ourselves, this negative energy is converted into physical and emotional malaise. This serves no useful purpose. All of the exercises explored in this chapter will help you to release your past shame, forgive yourself, and move forward in your life.

Think back to a mistake you've made in an earlier part of your life. If you could go back in time and change it, would you? _____. If you have answered "yes," this shows personal growth. Life experiences force us to learn from our mistakes, grow, and change. Behavior that we thought was perfectly acceptable at 20, sounds immature and just plain dumb when we are 40. That's just a part of our learning journey. We experience life moving forward, but we only learn through hindsight. (Yes, I know that this can be frustrating.)

As you learn to tame and take charge of this inner critic, you might be amazed at how differently you will begin to feel. Our self-talk profoundly influences our emotions and our physical well-being. This is why awareness is an important step in helping us to take charge of the messages that we are giving ourselves. In the chapter "Seeking Forgiveness from Others," you will be guided through the process of making apologies, amends, and restitution. For now, forgive yourself for being an imperfect person. Berating yourself is no longer an option!

8

THE FORGIVENESS STEPS

*I clutched certain resentments for two decades.
Wasted time. Wasted energy. Wasted hours,
that certainly could have been put to better use.
175,200 hours, to be exact!*

Have you ever said to yourself, "I know that this grudge is only hurting *me*, but I just can't find it in my heart to forgive?" When we feel hurt and offended, we can't see beyond our own pain. Sometimes, in spite of our best efforts, we just cannot bring ourselves to forgive a particular person.

We all know that it isn't healthy to harbor resentments, and most of us would probably advise a friend that it would benefit them to let go and move on with their lives. Yet, it can be difficult to follow our own advice.

In this chapter we will go from "talking the walk" to "walking the talk." My mother would often say that "actions speak louder than words," and this chapter is all about action! Before you begin this step, please remind yourself that forgiveness is for *you* and not for the offender. Take a deep breath. In your mind's eye, visualize inhaling courage. As you exhale, picture releasing any feelings of anxiety or fear.

(Please note that there is a separate chapter for parental forgiveness. This is because our relationships with our parents are unique, and differ from our other relationships. Thus, the forgiveness process is somewhat different. Please refer to Chapter 12 for the steps involved in forgiving your parents.)

STEP 1: PREPARATION

The first step should be handwritten, so you will need loose leaf paper or a notebook. When you write instead of type, this action engages your brain differently, and allows you to feel emotionally attached to the words you express. If you begin to feel resistant or angry as you are working through these steps, refer back to this sentence: "We are all imperfect people, and we make mistakes." This anchor will help you to refocus and soften your heart.

STEP 2: THE LIST

Write down the names of those who have offended you, and whom you've not forgiven. Next to each name, rate the degree of hurt caused by this individual's behavior. Use a scale of 1 to 10, where number 1 would indicate the least amount of pain, while the number 10 would imply that the offense and its consequences were devastating.

NAME | RATE OF HURT

_____ | _____
_____ | _____
_____ | _____
_____ | _____
_____ | _____
_____ | _____
_____ | _____

STEP 3: QUESTIONNAIRE FORM

Answer these questions for each person on your list. These reflective questions will help you to gain a deeper understanding of your feelings concerning each individual. There are additional forms in the appendix.

What was your relationship like prior to this event?

_____

_____

_____

What did each person say or do to offend you?

_____

_____

_____

How did it make you feel? (Try to be specific in identifying your feelings.)

_____

How has this offense negatively influenced your life?

Has the offense created an ongoing issue?

How has it impacted upon your relationship with yourself?

In what ways has it influenced your relationship(s) with others?

What is your relationship with the offending person like now?

Do you feel that you must receive an apology before you can forgive? _____

Any additional thoughts and feelings concerning this individual?

STEP 4: WRITE A LETTER

Using the answers to the questions in the third step, share your feelings in the form of a letter. The letter format will help you to explain how you feel, and how that person's behavior has negatively impacted upon your life. This is your chance to vent all of your anger and pain. (This letter should not be mailed!)

STEP 5: RELEASING EXPECTATIONS

Expectations are not our friends. When we expect others to behave according to our rules, and consistent with our ethics, we are going to be disappointed. When we're offended, our biggest expectation is to receive an apology! We feel that we deserve this, at the very least. Some of whom I've spoken to will not forgive their offender unless that person apologizes and expresses remorse. Due to this expectation, they have reached an impasse. They're stuck.

Consider this: If someone has offended you, there is the possibility that they have little regard for your feelings to begin with. If they had no misgivings about hurting you, why would they consider apologizing to you? Moreover, there are some offenses that an apology will not heal, and there are some people who will not apologize, even if they feel that they were wrong.

If we see an apology as a mandatory prerequisite for forgiveness, we are giving the offender power over our lives and our choices. If we want to move past our hurt, we need to forgive for *our* benefit, without expectations.

List some of your expectations for those who have offended you.

_____

_____

_____

_____

_____

STEP 6: IDENTIFY THE LEARNING OPPORTUNITY

We can convince ourselves that we have bad luck, or we can see adversity as a learning opportunity. If we choose the first, we are placing ourselves in the helpless victim role. If we choose the latter, we can use what we have learned as an opportunity for personal growth. In this step, list one or two lessons that you might have learned as a result of each offense.

_____

_____

_____

STEP 7: CHOOSE TO FORGIVE AND LET GO

In this step, we make a conscious choice to forgive for *our* benefit. In doing so, we release the pain and distress that connects us—binds us—to this offending individual. This process will give us freedom and relief that we cannot experience any other way. What do we lose? Our anger, resentment, chronic emotional pain, self-pity, and our victim stories. However, we regain control of our lives, our time, our energy, and ultimately… ourselves.

STEP 8: PERFORM THE LETTING-GO RITUAL

This symbolic and powerful step closes to the door to the past, and opens the door to the future. Gather any paperwork or notes that you have written, set them on fire, or tear them to shreds. Watch all of the painful words and feelings going up in flames. The vision of discarding these cumbersome feelings and letting go completely, will help to heal your heart. Now, you have earned and deserve the transformational impact of forgiveness.

CLOSING THOUGHTS

It took a lot of work to complete my forgiveness journey, and when I finished, I saw new beginnings and new possibilities that previously eluded me. As mentioned before, my life transformed, and yours can, too.

Do you feel like a burden has been lifted? _____.

If yes, enjoy this feeling, and envision giving yourself a great big hug! You deserve it.

9

FORGIVING YOUR SIBLINGS

*Clinging to childhood roles can negatively
influence our adult sibling relationships.*

Sometimes it can be more challenging to forgive family members, including siblings, than those who are not related to us, and don't share a family history. According to a survey conducted by Oakland University, 16% of respondents described their sibling relationships as adversarial. Another study found that 5-10% of the siblings interviewed were estranged. Why are difficulties in sibling relationships? Let's explore this, beginning with some questions.

Do you have a difficult relationship with one or more of your siblings? _____.

Do you share any common interests aside from your shared history? _____.

Do you feel guilty about any negative feelings you have toward this sibling? _____.

Are you experiencing ongoing struggles? _____.

These are difficult questions, and there aren't any easy answers, especially if you truly care about your siblings. The pressure to get along with siblings is further accentuated by the belief that family bonds are important—even essential.

CHILDHOOD ROLES

Clinging to our childhood roles can negatively influence our adult sibling relationships. For example, if you were a scapegoat or the "black sheep" in your family-of-origin, one or more of your siblings might still relate to you within the confines of this role. If this happens, it will compromise the success of your current relationship.

RECOGNIZING UNHEALTHY CHILDHOOD ROLES

In order to survive, children are often forced to assume certain roles in unhealthy families. Below is a synopsis: The *caretaker* assumes the adult responsibilities as well as the roles of one or both of the parents. These children are forced to be adults at a young age, so they miss out on the carefree joys of childhood.

The *hero* is in denial concerning the dysfunction, and truly believes that there aren't any problems within the family. This denial is a defense mechanism that protects the child.

The *scapegoat* is fully aware of the family discord, and will vocalize the problems to the other family members at every opportunity, often in a rebellious manner. Moreover, they are usually blamed for any problem that occurs within the family. These children are frequently frustrated that no one else recognizes the dysfunction.

The *clown* is the peacemaker. These children attempt to calm family conflicts through the use of humor. Some children also assume this role to get attention from their parents.

The *lost child* finds comfort and safety in being invisible and unnoticed. These children are very passive and quiet. Their goal is to hide in plain sight.

The *manipulator* has learned to cope by creating chaos. In this way, they are in control of the disruption, and, at the same time, they are redirecting the family away from the real dysfunction.

Can you recognize yourself in one of these roles? _____.

If yes, which one?

_____

_____

Can you recognize any of your siblings in one or more of these roles? _____.

If yes, which ones?

_____

_____

_____

_____

FAMILY HISTORY

It's not uncommon for different siblings to have different versions of their childhood history. This occurs more often if there was dysfunction, chaos, violence, abuse, alcoholism, or other addictions in the family. If so, denial might be the only way to protect themselves from unpleasant memories. If one of your siblings is in denial about your family-of-origin dysfunction, this can create ongoing friction in your relationship. We need to understand that, from their point of view, they truly have a different interpretation of the past.

As frustrating as this can be, you will not be able to convince them that your view is more accurate. The only solution is to *agree to disagree*, and consider further discussions on this topic to be off-limits. No one can win this battle.

Focusing on the present is the healthiest way to sustain adult sibling relationships. If you are currently working on your unresolved childhood issues, you cannot expect your siblings to validate your feelings or to help you on this journey. The smartest choice is to seek support from a counselor and other people in your life, and avoid this conversation with your siblings. We can't force others to see a situation or a memory through our eyes.

On a scale of 1 to 10, how frustrated would you be if one or more of your siblings did not share the same version of your childhood memories? _____.

Name one step that you could take to lessen your frustration.

_____

_____

Will you make a commitment to stop discussing your unresolved childhood conflicts with your siblings? _____.

AVOIDING GOSSIP

Gossip is so tempting when we feel frustrated and all other attempts at communication have failed. We might begin a conversation with the intention of seeking support, and before we realize it, our anger and frustration get the best of us, and we find ourselves besmirching our siblings. This is a good time to say to ourselves, "Stop!"

Gossip isn't a solution, but rather, an accelerant which only fuels the fire. Eventually your comments will get back to your sibling. (On some level, you might be hoping that this will happen.) If you have a problem with a sibling, avoid gossip. Attempt to have an honest conversation with your sibling.

If applicable, will you make a commitment to avoid gossip? _____.

BENDING AND BREAKING

We are usually far more cautious and restrained in family relationships, than we might be with friendships. We tolerate more toxicity, simply because the individual is a relative. We might attempt to avoid confrontation by ignoring offenses, relenting to the offending sibling, or assuming the blame. This unhealthy approach is unsustainable, and will eventually backfire. When we try to stuff our painful feelings, they will eventually impact upon our emotional and physical health. In the musical *Fiddler on the Roof*, the main character, Tevye struggled, but eventually forgave his two daughters for breaking tradition, and choosing their own spouses without a matchmaker. In the process, he experienced a great deal of anguish *twice*. However, when his third daughter broke tradition, by secretly marrying outside of the faith, although he struggled, he couldn't forgive her, saying: "If I bend this far, I will break."

If we continue to relent (bend) in a relationship, for the sake of family harmony, this will deplete us of self-respect. Healthy sibling relationships cannot survive with ongoing imbalance, and one-sided compromise.

Have you ever been in a situation where you relented or assumed the blame for the sake of peace, even though you felt that you were right? _____.

Please share the details:

_____

_____

_____

How did this make you feel?

_____

_____

_____

What was the resolution?

_____

_____

_____

_____

INHERITANCE DISPUTES

I touched upon this topic in my first book, and I'm including it in this workbook because it's more common that you might realize, and has the explosive potential to destroy sibling relationships and create life-long resentments.

According to a research study conducted by Ameriprise, 15% of adult siblings report conflicts over money, and nearly 70% of sibling money quarrels primarily focus on inheritance disparity-related issues. Only 33% of these issues get settled, and 28% remain unresolved.

Sometimes the disparity is the result of *undue influence* on the part of one of the siblings, which causes the other siblings to feel betrayed. For example, if a particular sibling was omitted from the Last Will & Testament without an adequate explanation as to why, this can raise suspicions. A second example might be a situation where a sibling took care of the parent, or a parent was financially dependent upon one of the siblings, and consequently, this sibling received more than the others. This could mean that the sibling influenced the decision of the parent who has created the *Will*.

Inheritance disputes often result in family battles or estrangement, and they can re-kindle past sibling rivalry and envy, during a sensitive and emotionally-charged time, when the siblings are also grieving the loss of their parent. If left unsettled, the hurt and the resentment can linger long after the relationship has ended. It can be painful to face the reality that a sibling could behave in this manner, but healing won't happen until you do so. It's also important to recognize that you have done nothing to deserve this treatment.

Have you experienced a disparity in terms of parental inheritance? _____.

If applicable, describe the situation.

_____

_____

_____

_____

What was the outcome?

_____

_____

_____

Have you forgiven this sibling? _____.

Have you reconciled? _____.

If not, are you willing to forgive your sibling, and release the resentment, even if reconciliation is not possible? _____.

WARNING SIGNS

In this section, we're going to explore some of the warning signs of unhealthy sibling relationships. Often, these patterns began in childhood. As mentioned earlier, if you've had a particular role during your childhood years, your family members might continue to relate to you within the context of this role.

Is the relationship one-sided?

If one sibling is doing all of the *giving*, and the other is doing all of the *taking*, then the relationship is unbalanced and unhealthy. Eventually you will begin to feel that you are being taken advantage of. You might even blame yourself for tolerating this behavior. The situation might be corrected by bringing this to the person's attention and re-establishing boundaries.

Have you been given "the silent treatment"?

In some ways, the *silent treatment* can be more hurtful and damaging than overt abuse and threats. When someone is purposely ignoring you, they're giving you the clear message that, as far as they're concerned, you don't exist, or you have absolutely no value as a person. This is the epitome of disrespect, and it can be difficult or nearly impossible to reconcile after you have been treated this way.

Is your relationship a series of tornadoes?

We will explore *trauma-drama addicts* in different chapter. For our purposes here, those addicted to chaos experience euphoria by orchestrating disasters. Often, this behavior is learned from childhood experiences in dysfunctional families. If you happen to be caught in the path of the other person's storm, you're in trouble. Most of us don't want disruption in our lives. Life can be challenging enough without unnecessary drama. If you have a sibling who is inclined to creating unnecessary drama, then, at the very least, remaining in this relationship will require a fair amount of distance.

Is there rivalry or jealousy?

Childhood sibling jealousy and rivalry can follow us into adulthood. Those who are envious live their lives in a chronic state of discontent, because they're constantly focused upon what others have, and what they lack. If sibling jealousy escalates, then this needs to be addressed directly, because the underlying tension will breed resentments.

Do you have a sibling relationship that includes any of the above warning signs? _____.

If yes, please explain:

_____
_____
_____

What steps have you taken to mend this situation?

_____
_____
_____
_____
_____

What was the outcome?

_____
_____
_____
_____
_____

WHEN ALL ELSE FAILS

It can be draining to attempt to mend a toxic sibling relationship, especially when disruption is ongoing. If you have tried to maintain a healthy relationship, but your sibling keeps sabotaging your efforts, it might be time to exit this relationship. Nothing can be resolved unless both individuals are willing to compromise and see the other person's perspective. Keep in mind that it is difficult and complicated to sever ties with family members. Not only is your sibling involved, but the rest of your family will be affected by this decision. Before deciding to walk away from this relationship, it might be wise to make a last attempt to sit down, face-to-face, and discuss your differences and points of contention. If this doesn't happen, then you will need to seriously consider proceeding to this last resort. Before finalizing this decision, however, it would be helpful to speak with your other family members, especially your other siblings, your parents, or your children.

CLOSING THOUGHTS

Forgiveness and reconciliation are possible if both siblings are willing to release childhood roles, be respectful, let go of the past, and possibly agree to disagree.

Here are some tips:

- Mutually agree to abide by certain ground rules.
- Recognize that it's okay to have opposing views.
- Be open to hearing your sibling's point of view.
- Listen, without being defensive.
- Avoid the blame game.
- Agree that you will disagree about certain issues.
- Agree that some topics are off limits, and honor this agreement.
- Re-establish boundaries.
- If estranged, ask a neutral third-party to moderate the conversation.
- Consider limited contact before completely exiting the relationship.

Forgiveness is important for *your* emotional well-being. If you're able to work out your differences, that would be ideal. If you have exhausted all options and you have decided to sever ties, try to let go of any residual resentment that you might still have, and know that you have tried your best.

10

FORGIVING YOUR CHILDREN

*Parenting requires an enormous amount of patience,
tolerance, energy, and a forgiving heart.*

IN MY WORK, I have heard many sad stories from parents who had difficult relationships with their adult children. Some of the parents were estranged from their children, and others seemed to have ongoing conflicts. This is particularly prevalent in mother-daughter relationships. When there is friction in a parent-child relationship, it's a sad situation for all involved. The parents have their version of the story, while the children might have a different perspective. However, although they both feel disappointment and hurt, often neither one is willing to just sit down and talk. Why? We can be stubborn when our egos get in our way, even when it's to our detriment.

In this chapter, we will explore this issue from the perspective of the parent, and look at some solutions that were shared by those who were able to resolve their differences with their children. Since I had a difficult relationship with my own mother, I get it. I also know how painful and heartbreaking it was for me during those times when we were estranged, and I am sure that it was difficult for her as well. In hindsight, I think that the need to be right, and the feelings of disappointment and hurt, overshadowed the feelings of love that we had for one another, and stubbornness didn't help. This scenario was common in many of the stories that others have shared with me.

Since I don't have children (unless you want to include my fur babies), I don't know first-hand what it feels like to have and raise children. However, from what I've been told, parenting requires an enormous amount of patience, tolerance, energy, and a forgiving heart.

Some of the most common scenarios included the following:

ROLE MODELS

No one is born knowing how to be a parent. It is a learned skill as well as an art. Parents usually learn parenting from their own parents, and refine these skills through trial and error. Like any new skill, there is often a learning curve.

If one's parents weren't particularly good role models, or there was stress in their family-of-origin, this will influence their parenting. Unhealthy parenting is often passed down through the generations, until someone breaks the cycle.

DOUBLE STANDARDS

Some parents said that imposing different rules for their sons and their daughters has created problems. Although this has changed in recent times, some cultures still adhere to these double standards. This can ignite culture clashes brought about by generational differences.

MOTHERING OR SMOTHERING?

There is a fine line between love and control. Obviously, parents will always worry about their children, even when the children become adults. However, sometimes being overly protective can make adult children feel as if they're being smothered. This situation can cause the children to become defensive and resentful.

MARITAL DIFFICULTIES

If the parents are having problems in their marriage, this impacts upon their children. Younger children may begin to feel insecure and afraid, and their security and stability is threatened. Marital difficulties can create stress for all family members. Some children feel angry, and might act out, or get into trouble. Many children blame themselves for the discord between their parents.

WHEN CHILDREN ARE TROUBLED

Parents who have troubled children experience an array of feelings. Some blame themselves and feel that they have failed as parents. Others feel unappreciated, become angry, and feel disappointed with the child. The reactions vary according to the age of the troubled child and the particular circumstances.

Some parents have shared that they were enablers, and this only made a bad situation worse. However, they were only able to recognize this in hindsight. Others chose to address the situation with a tough-love approach.

Depending upon the severity of the issue, some parents have told me that their relationships with their children caused them to live in a constant state of anxiety and worry.

DISAGREEMENTS

Different generations view life differently, and children are going to disagree with their parents. In these situations, being open-minded and respecting differences should always be the chosen path for both the parents and the children. Sometimes the best solution is to agree to disagree and respect differences.

JEALOUSY

Sibling jealousy and rivalry can also create disruption within the family. This is more prevalent when the siblings are the same gender. How many children have felt that one or both parents favored their sibling? Favoritism can cause conflicts between the children and their parents. Sometimes this can be subtle and on an unconscious level. Many parents have shared that when they became aware of jealousies, they discussed this with their children to ease their insecurities.

DISAPPROVAL

Sometimes parents disapprove of their child's chosen friends or love interests, and this can easily create friction. If the child is an adult, they are going to take offense, especially if it involves their significant other. No one likes to be judged or criticized, especially by their parents.

Have you ever had a resentment toward one or more of your children? _____.

Explain:

_____
_____
_____
_____
_____

How did this feel?

_____
_____
_____

How was this resolved?

_____
_____

CLOSING THOUGHTS

Here are some words of wisdom shared by parents who had forgiveness issues with their children:

"As difficult as it might be, it's best to take the initiative in making attempts toward reconciliation."

"I learned that I had to accept my son's choices, even when I didn't agree with them."

"Even though it's not easy, we need to let our kids to learn from their own mistakes."

"Sometimes we have to avoid giving our opinion."

Most of the interviewees said that they could not hold a grudge against their children for long. The estrangement was too upsetting. They have forgiven their children, even if they were not at fault, and their feelings had been hurt. Many had a conversation with their children to share how they felt about the discord. Others have moved forward without bringing up the past.

11

FORGIVING YOUR SPOUSE OR LIFE PARTNER

Forgiveness is the key to relationship longevity and success.

When several couples were interviewed and asked how they managed to keep their intimate relationships happy and satisfying, nearly all of them cited forgiveness, and understanding, as the qualities necessary for relationship longevity. Every couple also asserted that, although there were times of disagreement, they needed to learn how to resolve these situations through compromise. According to researcher Michael Rosenfeld, the majority of breakups occur within the first two years. After five years, only 20% of couples broke up. The longer a couple stays together, the less likely they are to end the relationship.

What steps do you take to resolve disagreements with your significant other?

_____
_____
_____
_____

Do you find it difficult to apologize or admit that you have been wrong? _____

What is one action that you can take today to work on this?

_____
_____
_____

UNRESOLVED GRUDGES

If we don't resolve our resentful feelings, they are still controlling us. When this happens, a small disagreement can be blown completely out of proportion, because we haven't let go of past resentments.

Jot down two ways in which you can resolve your grudges to reach a state of forgiveness.

_____

_____

_____

COMPARTMENTALIZATION

Although we love our significant others, there will be times when we become upset about something they have said or done. When this happens, it helps to separate your significant other's behavior from the love that you feel toward them.

List some of the qualities that you love about your significant other.

_____

_____

_____

RESPECTFULLY EXPRESSING YOURSELF

When we are upset, it's important to be aware of the way in which we express our thoughts. Using words like "I feel," rather than "You did," will allow your partner to be more responsive and less defensive. If we react with blame, our spouse or partner will instinctively stop listening.

List two sentences that you can use to approach your partner when you're angry with them, or you're both angry with one another, that doesn't put all the blame on them.

_____

_____

_____

DENIAL

When we pretend that we're not offended, or that nothing happened, resentments still exist just below the surface. One day, our spouse or partner might say something that irritates us, and we will unload all of the anger we have built up against them. We might be able to convince others that we aren't offended, but we can't deny our feelings to ourselves. It's better to address our resentments as quickly as possible.

Do you stuff your feelings and allow them to accumulate? _____

Can you make a commitment to share your feelings with your spouse or partner, instead of pushing them down? _____

OWNING YOUR PART

Most of us would prefer to think that arguments or disagreements aren't ever our fault. The reality is we all have our irritable moments. Take responsibility for your part in the discord, and apologize if it was your fault. The apology will help your partner to let go of any lingering hurt or anger.

Give two examples of what you might say to assume responsibility for your part in an argument.

_____
_____
_____
_____
_____
_____

WE'RE ALL DOING THE BEST WE CAN

Do you believe that you're doing the best you can, according to the resources available to you? _____

It helps to remember this when we are the offended person.

PRACTICE MAKES EASIER

The more that we practice forgiveness, the easier it gets. Keep in mind that forgiveness takes time and involves letting go of those things over which we have no control.

Let's look at control more closely…

List some things that you can't control which bother you.

_____
_____
_____
_____

How do you usually react when you don't have control over a situation?

_____
_____
_____
_____

The following is a list of suggested actions for maintaining healthy, long-term relationships. Notice how they reflect some aspect of kindness and forgiveness.

- Pause rather than speak in anger.
- Reverse roles to see your partner's point of view.
- Take a time-out when agitated, so you can calm down.
- Pay attention to your loved one.
- Choose your battles wisely
- Cultivate tolerance and empathy.
- Own your behavior.
- Apologize and accept apologies.
- Don't go to sleep angry.
- Leave the past in the past.
- Compromise.
- Forgive.

If you have others, share below.

_____
_____
_____
_____

List any of the suggested actions that you struggle with.

_____
_____
_____

Are you willing to work on these areas? _____.

WHEN THE RELATIONSHIP IS OVER

Sometimes, despite our best efforts, it might be time to part ways. It's very easy to be resentful when a relationship doesn't work out the way we expected. Unfortunately, many unsuccessful relationships leave both parties with unresolved conflicts, resentments, and unfinished business.

Are you battling with unresolved resentments following a breakup? _____

Are you obsessing over your victim story? _____

In hindsight, what lessons have you learned from this relationship?

_____

_____

_____

_____

_____

Are you willing to avoid repeating the same mistakes? _____

Jot down two mistakes that you've made in this relationship that you will not repeat.

_____

_____

_____

CLOSING THOUGHTS

All intimate relationships require ongoing work and effort, and forgiveness is the key to longevity and success. Regardless of our decision to remain in the relationship or sever ties, the healthiest way to use our energy is to forgive, move forward, and carry on with our lives.

12

FORGIVING YOUR PARENTS

Forgiving our parents is the epitome of forgiveness.

THIS CHAPTER WILL ASSIST YOU IF YOU NEED TO FORGIVE one or both of your parents, and help you to close the door on the past. This topic has special meaning to me for a few reasons. First, I struggled for decades to forgive my mom, and to understand the underlying dynamics of our relationship. In fact, the writing of my first book, *The Forgiveness Journey: Transcend Your Hurt, Transform Your Life*, began with an introspective search into this relationship, and, in being able to forgive her, the inspiration to write my first, and this second book. I was tired of the pain of chronic resentment that I had toward her, which went on for decades, and continued to live on, even after her passing. This exploration led me on a journey to release this resentment. After viewing the world through her eyes, and completing all of the steps that I share in this chapter, I was finally able to feel the love that I've always had toward her. For the first time, I saw her as just another flawed person, like myself, separate from the unfulfilled expectations and the disappointments that I've had toward her throughout my life. These insights caused my resentment to melt away, which transformed my life.

Then I continued with this work, deeply exploring every aspect of forgiveness, and I forgave everyone else in my life. Ultimately, forgiving my mother started me on this journey, and inspired me to write these two books.

If you're working on this chapter, then I assume that you've experienced some difficulties with your parents as a child, or are still struggling now. Perhaps your parents have passed away and you still have some unfinished business. If this is so, you can still work through these steps and forgive them.

Both of my parents have passed away decades ago, but I was still able to forgive them. However, it took many years before I felt ready to do so. Do you remember what I shared earlier? "I embraced certain resentments for two decades, 175,200 hours, to be exact! Wasted time, wasted energy." When I forgave my parents, and then everyone else, my life completely changed. I was able to transcend my hurt and transform my life. This is my wish for you! Forgiving our parents is different from forgiving others in our lives. We are presented with a unique set of challenges as well as a splendid healing opportunity. Our parental relationships are unique because we have expectations of them that exceed our expectations of others.

We were dependent upon them for our survival as children. We counted on them to protect and nurture us. We may have wanted them to be flawless, perhaps even superheroes. We may have watched TV shows depicting perfect moms and dads, and wanted our parents to live up to those standards. These expectations make parental forgiveness delicate and complex. Moreover, we might need to forgive a lifetime of disappointments rather than one specific incident.

Because of the specific challenges involved in forgiving parents, this unique act of forgiveness can make it easier to forgive anyone else. Parental forgiveness softens our hearts and opens them to new possibilities. Here's a brief look at my own story.

"Why can't she be different?" This was the ongoing question I had about my mother when she was alive. It never occurred to me that the feeling might have been mutual. I wanted her to meet my expectations of what a mother should be, and was disappointed when she couldn't live up to this standard. I wanted to have a close relationship with her, even though I made no effort on my part to do so. I always felt as if there was an invisible wall between us. However, I was unable to recognize that it was two-sided. Before I was able to fully forgive her, I had to recognize that she was simply an imperfect woman, just like me. In many ways, it's sad that I was not able to see this when she was still alive. Most of the time, I couldn't see beyond my disappointment in her.

As I was doing my forgiveness work, it suddenly struck me that she might have felt this same disappointment with me. I had to admit to myself that while I was judging her imperfections, I hadn't noticed that I was far from the perfect daughter. Wow! It hit me like a lightning bolt! I shed the tears of a lifetime, and faced the frozen grief that I was unable to feel when she passed away. This revelation was enlightening, shocking, painful, and, ultimately, liberating. There is a good chance that you might have a similar revelation, so brace yourself and have tissues nearby.

A large part of my forgiveness work involved seeing the world through my mother's eyes, and from the position of an adult woman, rather than a wounded child. In doing so, I was able to fully understand the challenges and the struggles that she endured with incredible courage.

TRANSFERENCE

Many of our current struggles are often a reflection of our unresolved parental issues. These fractured relationships can influence our relationships with our life partners, spouses, friends, employers, and even our children. Moreover, they can cause us to have adversarial feelings toward authority figures such as teachers, police, and employers. Obviously, this can create a lot disruption in our lives.

Do you have any relationships where the other person reminds you of one of your parents? _____.

If so, has this transference created difficulties? _____.

If yes, what are they?

_____

_____

_____

Do you have any difficulties with authority figures? _____.

If yes, write down specifics.

_____

_____

_____

_____

_____

STEP 1 - THE NARRATIVE

As mentioned earlier, we all have a story. Like us, our parents have also been shaped by the remnants of their history, their struggles, and their own stories. This first step is an important doorway on your parental forgiveness journey. You will be examining who they are (or were), through your eyes as an adult.

I spent a great deal of time writing, rewriting, and reflecting upon my mother's story. With each revision, I was able to understand her on a much deeper level. You might have a similar experience. I am sharing her story and my reflections, because I am hoping that some of my sentiments might resonate with you, and help you when you write your own narrative.

STEP ONE - MY MOTHER'S STORY

My mother was a beautiful woman. She was about 5'2", and had a light complexion, blonde hair, and beautiful, blue eyes. She looked exactly like her mother, except for her eye color. She loved jewelry, especially earrings, and she had a refined taste.

She always made sure that she looked her best, even though she struggled with being overweight. Every week she had her hair styled by a hairdresser. She looked forward to her appointments, and I think that they might have been the happiest part of her week. My mom had a lot of health problems, including the long-term consequences of rheumatic fever. She also had rheumatoid arthritis and cardiac problems, and she struggled with these medical issues throughout her life.

She was first-generation American, born of Italian immigrants, and she was bilingual. When she didn't want my sister and I to know what she was saying, she spoke to my father (who was also bilingual) in Italian. My grandfather was a hardworking brick mason, and my grandmother was a homemaker. My grandfather was an attractive man with hazel eyes, and my grandmother was a very pretty woman with light hair. Unfortunately, she was often ill, and she suffered from severe hypertension. Sadly, she lived during a time before blood pressure medications existed. Still, she was fondly remembered as a kind and sweet woman, and a loving mother, who took good care of her family.

From what I was told, my grandmother loved nurses, because she was chronically ill, and was grateful for the loving care that they gave her. Therefore, she and my grandfather sacrificed and saved what little money they had, so that they could send one of their daughters to nursing school.

My grandmother passed away at the young age of 47, and although my grandfather was a young widower, he never remarried. I know that my mom never quite recovered from the premature death of her own mother, because she often spoke about her mom, and how much she missed her. I remember her listening and crying to a song called "Mama". I'm sure that this loss had an enormous impact upon her life.

Like many parents during that era, my grandparents were strict with their children and especially protective of their daughters. My mother often shared this story concerning a curfew she had when she was a teenager. She went on a date and saw the movie *Gone with the Wind*, but she had to leave before the movie was over, since her curfew was at 10 pm. It always bothered her that she never saw the end of that movie. One day, I noticed that the movie was scheduled to be on television, so I watched it to the end on her behalf. It wasn't my favorite movie, and it was quite long, but I watched the entire film in honor of her, and her unfulfilled wish to see it to its conclusion.

My mom was married at the age of 19. From what I was told, she and my father really wanted children, but they had difficulties conceiving. I have heard stories that my mom would often cry, because she desperately wanted to be a mother. After ten years of marriage, since they felt that they would not be able to have biological children, they adopted me. Then, two years later, my mother became pregnant, and she gave birth to my sister.

Through the eyes and the memory of a child, I remember that there was a great deal of stress and friction in our household, and my parents were constantly anxious about their financial situation. Due to my father's gambling issues, which led to further financial difficulties, my mother was eventually forced to go back to work. This was very difficult and stressful for her, because she had so many medical issues. Despite this, she went to work every day. Although my mother went to high school, she did not have any work-related experience, so she could not find a white collar job working in an office. The only job that she was qualified for was that of a seamstress. She was very talented, and she also had a talent for crochet and knitting. To make ends meet, in her spare time, she would crochet and knit beautiful items, and sell these locally. My parents had a lot of pride, and they believed that you should never ask anyone for financial assistance. I, personally, still share this philosophy. Working as a seamstress was not a glamorous job. The working conditions were atrocious. She worked in a sweat-shop, doing piecework, and paid for each piece of clothing she assisted in making. There was no air conditioning, and it was brutally hot during the summer months. She was an intelligent woman, and had a particular knack for arithmetic. She could add and subtract numbers in lightning speed in her head. Sadly, I am sure her career as a seamstress was not the life that she had envisioned for herself.

When my sister and I were teenagers, my father became seriously ill and passed away. The survivor social security benefits were minimal, and he did not have life insurance. Ultimately, my mom was forced to sell our house to pay his enormous hospital bills, and we had to relocate to a three-room apartment. Consequently, we had to discard many of our belongings. The transition hit us hard. We all felt lost. It was an upsetting time, filled with sorrow, fear, uncertainty, and numerous adjustments. At the young age of 47, my mother must have been a very frightened widow. However, she never vocalized her fears. She was suddenly solely responsible for raising two teenage daughters with limited funds. She must have been terrified.

It's interesting to note that my grandmother died at the age of 47. I think that, in many ways, as my mother's world began to crumble, a big part of her died at the exact same age as her mother. Sometimes you can still be alive, but not fully living.

My mother could be somewhat stoic at times, she had difficulties in expressing affection and often hid her feelings. It was easier for her to express anger and frustration, than hurt or disappointment. Now I can see that this was a form of self-defense—a survival mechanism and a way to protect herself and her vulnerabilities. At times, she did show her more sensitive side, and would share how easily her feelings were hurt.

My mother remarried for companionship when she was 56 years old. When she was 73, she had a cerebral hemorrhage, had unsuccessful surgery, and was in the hospital for seven weeks before she passed away. There was a lot of family disruption and estrangement after her death, because her last wishes were not honored. Those details are unimportant here. What is important is to share that, although she and I had our disagreements, we got along much better during her final years.

A Funny Family Memory

My grandfather came from an era and a culture which frowned upon women who smoked cigarettes. Smoking was considered inappropriate for women, and there was a social stigma associated with women who smoked. So, he had no idea that all of his daughters smoked. Since they didn't want to upset him, my mother and her sisters would hide this from him. Keep in mind that they were adults and married women.

I remember times when they were smoking, and would hear him coming into the house, so they would run into the bathroom to discard their cigarettes. The whole family thought that this was hilarious.

Post-Forgiveness Insights

After forgiving my mom, my feelings regarding her have drastically changed. Once upon a time, I would feel anxiety when she phoned me, because there was the possibility of an argument, and we both became overly sensitive and defensive. *Now, I would give anything to hear her voice just one more time.* Every day, I look at her photo, send her my love, and tell her that I miss her. She passed away in 1997, yet there are still moments when I mourn the loss of what could have been—the possibility that we could have had a better relationship, one without friction or power struggles. We could have done so if both of us had let down our guard for a few seconds, to see the other as an imperfect woman, rather than a battle to be fought and won at all costs.

Perhaps you have had a combative relationship with one or both of your parents. Please know that although you can't change past, forgiveness will change your present and future. I urge you not to waste precious time ruminating about past offenses. After clearing away the grudges, I was able to remember a piece of wisdom that she would share with me: "You have to give yourself courage. No one can do it for you." These words continue to give me strength when I'm going through difficulties. Are our mothers perfect? No. Have they made mistakes? Almost certainly. If we resent our mothers, we won't be able to recognize any of their good qualities until we let that resentment go.

When I reflect upon my mother's life today, I can recognize and appreciate that she was a brave and courageous woman. Although the odds were against her, giving up was never an option. Now that's something to be admired! Even if you feel that your parents were the worst parents in the world, you will probably miss one or both of them when they're gone. I can tell you from my own experience, that if your parents die before you are able to forgive them, your unresolved resentments will torment you until you do so.

I hope that my sharing helps you to see that you are not alone. So many of us have grudges toward our mothers that can cause us a lifetime of grief. You have the power to change this now and avoid further suffering. It is important to write your parents' narrative without judgment. We will address the hurt and pain that you may have endured later on. Here are some reflective questions that will help you compose your mother's narrative. Like myself, you might be surprised to discover that you can't answer some of them, which raises the question, "How well do we really know our parents as people?"

Briefly describe your mother's appearance/physical characteristics.

_____
_____
_____
_____
_____

Was appearance important to her? ___

Check off any personality traits which apply.

- ___ Easygoing
- ___ Aggressive
- ___ Passive
- ___ Loving
- ___ Affectionate
- ___ Stoic
- ___ Nurturing
- ___ Strict
- ___ Controlling
- ___ Smothering
- ___ Easygoing

Others:

_____
_____
_____
_____

What made her angry?

_____
_____
_____
_____

What made her happy?

_____
_____
_____
_____

What made her sad?

_____
_____
_____
_____

Our cultural backgrounds can define us in powerful ways, and can influence how we raise our children.

Do you see a connection between her culture and her parenting? _____ If so, how?

_____
_____
_____
_____

If she had both, did she have different rules for her sons versus her daughters? _____ If yes, your thoughts?

_____
_____
_____

Just as you were influenced by your mother, her parents were influential in her life too. In a few words, and to the best of your recollection, describe your maternal grandparents.

_____
_____
_____

What was your mother's childhood like? (Answer to the best of your ability.)

Were there alcohol or addiction problems in her family of origin?
_____

Were her parents strict or liberal?
_____

Did her parents have a good relationship with one another?
_____

Where there financial difficulties?
_____

Were there any serious medical issues? _____. If yes, describe.
_____
_____

Were there any mental health issues? _____. If yes, describe.
_____
_____
_____

What were her relationships with her siblings like, if she had them?
_____
_____

Did they get along with one another? _____ If there was friction, describe.
_____
_____

Where was she educated?
_____
_____

What was her occupation?

_____

_____

Did she like her job? _____

How would you describe the relationship between you mother and your father?

_____

_____

_____

_____

What were her possible stresses or insecurities?

_____

_____

_____

_____

From the questions you've answered, write your mother's story in narrative form. (You can exclude anything that you feel might be unnecessary.) Wait at least 24 hours, and then re-read it, aloud if possible. Before you begin, try to pretend that you're reading a story about someone you do not know. You might be surprised at how much insight you gather as you read her story again. Feel free to revise or expand upon her story, if you feel a need to.

Post-Narrative Reflective Questions:

Jot down any random thoughts or feelings that arise after re-reading her story.

1. _____
2. _____
3. _____
4. _____

In writing your mother's narrative, is there anything which surprised you? If so, what?

_____
_____
_____

Has this step helped you to see her differently? If yes, in what ways?

_____
_____
_____
_____

STEP TWO—YOUR PAIN, DISAPPOINTMENT, AND ANGER

In this step, write down all of your pain, hurt, and disappointment, and all of your needs that you feel your mother did not meet.

Let's look at some common areas which might require your forgiveness:

All the ways she wasn't there for you

Did you feel neglected, misunderstood, ignored? If so, in what ways?

1. _____
2. _____
3. _____

Not spending more time with you? Give an example:

_____
_____

Not being more loving? Give an example:

_____
_____

Not recognizing your achievements? Give an example:

_____

_____

Not supporting you and guiding you? Give an example:

_____

_____

Any abuse or neglect? Give an example:

_____

_____

Criticisms and verbal abuse? Give an example:

_____

_____

Addictions? Give an example:

_____

_____

Mental illness? Give an example:

_____

_____

Weakness? Give an example:

_____

_____

Insensitivity or stoicism? Give an example:

_____

_____

Being a poor spouse to your other parent? Give an example:

_____

_____

Not taking the time to understand you? Give an example:

_____

_____

Not protecting you? Give an example:

_____

_____

List any others below:

1. _____
2. _____
3. _____

To create some balance, I'm going to play the devil's advocate with these questions. Please reflect upon these questions before continuing with the next steps:

Do you believe that anyone can live up to all of these expectations? _____

Can you identify with any of these issues in your role as a parent, if you are one? _____

If yes, which ones?

_____

_____

_____

_____

Post-Narrative Reflective Questions

Jot down any random thoughts or feelings that arise after re-reading this narrative.

_____

In writing her narrative, is there anything which surprised you? If so, what?

Has this step helped you to see her differently? _____ If yes, in what ways?

STEP THREE - THE LETTER

The letter format is designed to assist you in sharing your hurt in a personal way. After gathering your thoughts from the previous focus questions, and answering the following questions, you will share them in a letter format. (not to be mailed).

Before you can completely let go and forgive, it is important to express your hurt feelings.

Here are additional focus questions to guide you:

How has this parental relationship influenced your life?

How has it influenced your relationships with others?

In what ways has this influenced your relationship with yourself?

Write down any life lessons that you might have learned as a result of your relationship with your mother.

If she hurt you, recognize that what happened was not okay, and allow yourself to feel your negative emotions.

When writing your letter, say: *"I feel ..."* rather than *"You did..."*

Now, write your letter, beginning with *"Dear mom,"* or just *"Mom,"* After writing the letter, place two chairs opposite one another. Envision your mother sitting in the empty chair. Read your letter out loud. After doing so, either rip up the letter or burn it. This is the symbolic part of letting go, and it is powerful. (Do not save or mail the letter.)

STEP FOUR - THE IMAGINARY CONVERSATION
(Excerpt from The Forgiveness Journey)

In this step, you will have an imaginary conversation with your mother. Place two chairs facing each other four to five feet apart. If you have a photo, place it on the empty chair where your mother would be sitting. If you don't have a photo, this is okay. You will just need to use your imagination, and bring forth a mental image of her.

Imagine your mother sitting in the empty chair. Look into her eyes...

Imagine that you are able, just for a few moments, to see her as simply another person—a woman, who might have had her own struggles in life...

Listen to her, as she drops down her guard and shares her fears, her insecurities, and her own wounds...

Listen to her as she tells you that she loves you... how she has made some mistakes...

How she tried her best, despite of her limitations and in spite of her own hidden pain...

Hear her say that it was never your fault... that you were her beautiful child...

How she wishes that she could take away all of the pain that she caused you...

How she wants to understand how you feel...

Now open your heart and share your hurts, your disappointment, your anger...

Look into her eyes again... see the tears in her eyes, as she says:

"Please forgive me."

If you feel inclined, imagine giving her a hug. If not, that's okay too.

Now go to that place deep down inside you, where you feel love and compassion...

Make the choice to forgive her *for your own benefit,* and feel all of your pain melt away.

STEP ONE—YOUR FATHER'S STORY

Now it's time to write your father's story, and capture a glimpse of his world through his eyes. As with your mother's narrative, it is equally important to write his story without judgment. Later on, we will address the hurt and pain that you may have endured. Please know that this exercise is not about condoning any wrongdoing. It is designed to create a new level of understanding, by seeing the world as he might have experienced it.

Here are some reflective questions that will help you compose his narrative.

Briefly describe your father's appearance/physical characteristics.

_____

_____

_____

Was his appearance important to him? _____

Check off any personality traits which apply.

- ___ Easygoing
- ___ Aggressive
- ___ Passive
- ___ Loving
- ___ Affectionate
- ___ Stoic
- ___ Nurturing
- ___ Strict
- ___ Controlling
- ___ Smothering
- ___ Easygoing

Others:

_____
_____
_____

What made him angry?

_____
_____
_____

What made him happy?

_____
_____
_____

What made him sad?

_____
_____
_____

His Cultural Background

Our cultural backgrounds can define us in powerful ways and can influence how we parent our own children.

Do you see a connection between his culture and his parenting? If so, how?

_____

_____

_____

_____

If he had both, did he have different rules for male and female children? _____

Just as you were influenced by your father, his parents were also influential in his life.

In a few words, and to the best of your recollection, describe your paternal grandparents.

_____

_____

_____

What was your father's childhood like? (Answer to the best of your ability.)

Were there alcohol or addiction problems in his family of origin? _____

Were his parents strict or liberal? _____

Did his parents have a good relationship with one another? _____

Where there financial difficulties? _____

Were there any serious medical issues? _____. If yes, describe.

_____

_____

Were there any mental health issues? _____. If yes, describe.

_____

_____

What were his relationships like with his siblings, if he had any?

_____

_____

Did they get along with one another well? _____

Was there friction among his siblings? _____

Where was he educated?

_____

_____

What was his occupation? _____

Did he like his job? _____

How would you describe the relationship between you mother and your father?

_____

_____

_____

What were his possible stresses or insecurities?

_____

_____

_____

_____

From the questions you've answered, write your father's story in narrative form. You can exclude anything that you feel might be unnecessary.

After you have completed this step, wait at least twenty four hours, and then read his narrative. Reading it aloud will often increase the impact. I would like you to pretend you are reading a story about someone you do not know. You might be surprised at how much insight you gather as you re-read his story. Feel free to revise or expand upon it as necessary.

Post-Narrative Reflective Questions

Jot down any random thoughts or feelings that arise after re-reading his narrative.

_____
_____
_____

In writing his narrative, was there anything which surprised you? If so, what?

_____
_____
_____

Has this step helped you to see your father differently? ____ If yes, in what ways?

_____
_____
_____

STEP TWO—YOUR PAIN, DISAPPOINTMENT AND ANGER

In this step, write down all of your pain, hurt, and disappointment, and all of your needs that you felt were unmet by your father. Let's look at some common areas which might require your forgiveness.

All the ways he wasn't there for you

Did you feel neglected, misunderstood, ignored? In what ways?

_____
_____
_____
_____

Not spending more time with you? Give an example:

_____
_____

Not being more loving? Give an example:

_____
_____
_____

Not recognizing your achievements? Give an example:

_____
_____

Not supporting you and guiding you? Give an example:

_____
_____

Any physical abuse or neglect? Give an example:

_____
_____

Criticisms and verbal abuse? Give an example:

_____
_____

Addictions? Give an example:

_____
_____

Mental illness? Give an example:

_____
_____

Weakness? Give an example:

_____
_____

Insensitivity or stoicism? Give an example:
_____
_____

A poor spouse to your other parent? Give an example:
_____
_____
_____

Not taking the time to understand you? Give an example:
_____
_____
_____

Not protecting you? Give an example:
_____
_____

List any others below:
_____
_____
_____
_____

Can you identify with any of these issues in your role as a parent, if you are one? _____

If yes, which ones?
_____
_____
_____

STEP THREE - THE LETTER

The letter format is designed to help you in sharing your pain on a personal level. After gathering your thoughts in Step 2, you will share them in this letter format. Before you can completely let go and forgive, it is important to express your hurt feelings. Using the information in step 2, and the answers to the following questions, compose your letter.

How has your relationship with your father influenced your life?

_____
_____
_____
_____

How has it influenced your relationships with others?

_____
_____
_____
_____

How has it influenced your relationship with yourself?

_____
_____
_____
_____

Write down any lessons that you might have learned as a result of your relationship with your father.

_____
_____
_____
_____
_____

Begin the letter with *"Dear dad,"* or simply *"Dad,"* In writing your letter, say, *"I feel ..."* rather than *"You did..."* and avoid judgments. Recognize that if your father hurt you, that was not okay, and allow yourself to feel your negative emotions.

After writing the letter, imagine sitting opposite him. Now read the letter aloud. After doing so, either tear the letter to pieces, or burn it. This is the symbolic part of letting go, and it can powerful. (Do not mail the letter!)

STEP FOUR - THE IMAGINARY CONVERSATION

Place two chairs facing each other, and place your father's photo on the empty chair, if available.

In a quiet, comfortable place, where you will not be interrupted, begin this meditation…

Imagine your father sitting in the empty chair. Look into his eyes…

Imagine that you are able, just for a few moments, to see him as simply another person—a man, who might have experienced his own struggles…

Listen to him as he puts down his guard and shares his fears… his insecurities… his own wounds… perhaps his own struggles with trying to be a good father…

Listen as he tells you that he loves you… how he made some mistakes… failed…

How he tried his best, despite his limitations… and his own issues and hidden pain…

How he tried to be strong…

Hear him say that it was never your fault… that you were his beautiful child…

How he wishes that he could take away all of the pain that he caused you…

How he wants to understand how you feel…

Now open your heart and share your hurts, your disappointment, your anger…

Look into his eyes again. See his tears, as he says…

"I am so sorry. Please forgive me… I love you."

Now go to that place deep within you, where you feel love or compassion…

Make the choice to forgive him, and feel your pain melt away.

THROUGH THE EYES OF A CHILD

Before closing this chapter, I would like to share some final insights that helped me to forgive my parents. Please reflect upon these three questions, before you read the remainder of this chapter.

Do you see the world differently now than you did ten years ago? _____

How about twenty years ago? _____

Do you believe that you saw the world differently as a child? _____

When we are children, all of our experiences are filtered through our developmental level at the time. As we mature, hopefully, we begin to view life as an adult. Nevertheless, our childhood memories have been etched in our brains from a child's perspective. Moreover, some of our memories might lack clarity due to the passage of time.

When we transition from childhood to adulthood, we don't close one door and open another. We don't suddenly become 100% adult and 0% child. Some individuals never grow up, they just grow old. The rest of us are floating somewhere on the child-adult spectrum. Many of us tend to approach our painful childhood memories through the eyes of the child we once were. This doesn't invalidate our experiences and our pain. It is, however, worthy of a closer look.

A few years ago, I returned to my childhood neighborhood. I remembered my house as being huge. Viewing that same house as an adult, however, it looked so small. I was really surprised at the difference between my recollections and the reality. My perception was tainted by my perspective as a child. This old memory was invalidated when I saw this house through the eyes of an adult. And my point is? Perception is subjective, and not always 100% accurate, and our resentments can taint our perceptions in powerful ways. This point is worth reflection and consideration.

RECONCILIATION

If your parents are still alive and you're estranged, you have an opportunity to reconcile. Before doing so, I suggest a face-to-face conversation where you can assertively (not aggressively) let them know what you're not comfortable with in terms of your interactions with them. If they agree to respect your boundaries, then by all means, reconcile. I would also recommend that you share some of your insights with them if you feel comfortable.

CLOSING THOUGHTS

I know how challenging it can be to forgive parents and close the door on childhood issues. Forgiveness is a choice and readiness will be the fuel that ignites your journey. You need to recognize that you are ready to forgive for *your* benefit. Make the decision for *you*.

In doing so, you will be releasing your parents from the prison cell that you've been guarding for years (and putting your own life on hold to do so.) You'll be free and so will your offender. You will take your power back so you can move forward in your life.

Resentments love expectations, because it keeps them alive. Once you wave goodbye to your expectations, it will be easier to forgive and release resentment. Our primary expectation is usually the desire for an apology, because we think that this will soothe our pain. The last thing that we want to hear is "I did the best that I could," when we feel that their "best" simply was not good enough. Consider this… *Maybe,* just *maybe,* it *was* the best that they could do, given their limitations, their own unresolved wounds and issues, and the resources that were available to them at that time. That doesn't excuse any hurtful events, but it does offer an explanation and some insight.

In apologizing, your parents are essentially admitting that they have failed. It is a huge admission. They will likely have difficulties in conceding that they might not have been good parents. At the least, they may not have been the parent that you wanted, needed, and expected. That's one enormous apology! If you want to move forward and heal your heart, then your forgiveness cannot be contingent upon receiving an apology. The moment you stop expecting one, you will be able to complete your forgiveness journey and your life *will* get better.

I carried my childhood resentments into my adult life. These unresolved grudges tainted my adult relationship with my mother, and other relationships as well, especially with authority figures. If you are in this place, and your parents are still alive, I urge you to attempt an adult conversation. Many years ago I had an opportunity to do so with my mom, and I declined. I still regret that decision. Seize the opportunity.

13

FORGIVING CHRONIC OR SERIOUS ILLNESSES

*People can support us
and walk **with** us on our journey,
but no one can walk it **for** us.*

IT IS CHALLENGING TO LIVE WITH A CHRONIC OR A SERIOUS ILLNESS, because these life-changing situations can stir up many feelings that will need to be worked through. In this chapter, we will explore the various aspects of forgiveness, as they relate to serious medical issues. Since I am on peritoneal dialysis for chronic kidney disease, awaiting a transplant, and I live with chronic pain from other medical issues, this chapter has special significance for me. If you have a chronic or serious medical issue, you have probably experienced a wide range of emotions, including anxiety, fear, resentment, anger and self-pity. Your illness might require you to make lifestyle changes, or more frequent medical appointments. Since these changes create disruption and increase stress, it wouldn't be surprising if you have developed a resentment toward your illness.

In this chapter, we will walk through the steps that lead us to acceptance, insight, and forgiveness in terms of our illnesses. In reflecting upon and writing out these feelings, we can learn a lot about ourselves and measure our personal growth. I will never forget the moment when my nephrologist told me that I needed to be on dialysis. Even though I knew that my bloodwork indicated this, when the words came out of his mouth, I suddenly became overwhelmed with sadness and fear. I have other chronic illnesses and I live with chronic pain, and it can be frustrating, to say the least. However, this was different because it was life-threatening and serious. If you have a chronic or serious illness, you probably can identify with these feelings.

What illnesses are you dealing with?

_____

_____

Share any initial reactions that you can recall upon getting your diagnosis:

_____
_____
_____
_____

THE GRIEF PROCESS

There is an acute sadness that accompanies the news that we have an illness that isn't going away, might get worse, or can be life-threatening. Added to this, we might feel additional stress if we know that we might need surgery as a result of this illness. Before forgiving our illness, we need to grieve certain losses that it has created. All chronic illnesses are accompanied by lifestyle changes, new limitations, and losses that can feel similar to the loss of a loved one. Perhaps you find it difficult to make plans in advance because you can't predict how you will feel. You might not be able to engage in activities that you once enjoyed. Maybe you're frustrated by your increasing dependence on others as well as health care providers. These are all perceived as losses. Moreover, if your illness is life-threatening, this shocking reality forces you to face your own mortality. None of us relish reflecting upon our demise. Know that you can work through the grieving process and reach a point of acceptance and strength. Let's walk this path together.

SHOCK AND DENIAL

Even if you have a progressive illness, you will still likely experience shock and a certain amount of denial when your doctor tells you that it has gotten worse. I had chronic kidney disease for over a decade and I knew that it was progressing. Still, when my doctor told me that I needed to be on dialysis, I was stunned to actually hear these dreaded words. My first reaction was to blame my nausea and other symptoms on anything but the real cause. Perhaps you've had a similar initial reaction.

Can you remember the feelings and thoughts that you had during this stage?

_____
_____
_____
_____
_____

EMOTIONAL PAIN AND GUILT

As the shock fades, the emotional pain makes an appearance. Even though we would like to avoid the pain, the only way to get past it is to walk through it. Sometimes we blame ourselves if we think that we might have caused or contributed to our illness.

Share some of the feelings you've experienced during this period.

_____
_____
_____
_____

ANGER AND BARGAINING

Many of us become angry when we feel afraid or helpless. This defense is an attempt to protect us from emotional distress. There are few situations that can make us feel more helpless and angry than a serious medical diagnosis. Often, within an angry adult is a frightened child. Acknowledging this can help us to address our fears.

How do you react when you feel helpless?

_____
_____
_____

How do you behave when you're afraid?

_____
_____
_____

How do you address your anger?

_____
_____
_____

As desperation grows, some individuals bargain with the God of their understanding.

If you've done so, please jot down your experiences.

_____
_____
_____
_____
_____

REFLECTION AND DEPRESSION

As we begin to face reality, we might become depressed as we contemplate upon our new situation. I recall feeling like I was in a small boat being tossed around by stormy waters. I felt so helpless.

Can you remember your feelings during this stage?

_____
_____

THE LIFE ADJUSTMENT STAGE

During this stage, we begin to accept and adapt to our new circumstances. Our life begins to improve as our depression and hopelessness decrease.

Please jot down what you felt and experienced during this stage, if you have reached it.

_____
_____
_____
_____

ACCEPTANCE AND HOPE

Acceptance and hope are the final stages of grief. Acceptance doesn't necessarily include happiness. It simply means that we accept what we cannot change. During this period, we become comfortable with our new set of circumstances and take appropriate actions to live our best lives.

What are the steps that you took (or can take) to reach acceptance?

_____

_____

_____

What tools do you use to give yourself hope?

_____

_____

_____

FORGIVENESS

Having moved past the grieving process, we can address forgiving our medical challenges and explore the learning opportunities and lessons we can take with us from the experience. Initially, there will likely be a certain amount of resentment that we feel toward our illness. However, being powerless over our external circumstances forces us to find strength within ourselves. My mom would often say that when we are faced with challenges, we need to give ourselves courage. No one else can do this for us. So true! People can support us and walk *with* us on our journey, but no one can walk it *for* us.

During this period, our self-image may move away from feeling like a victim and toward feeling like an empowered survivor.

As an individual with a chronic or serious illness, how do you define yourself?

_____

_____

_____

LIFE LESSONS

Some might wonder, "What life lessons can a serious illness teach us?" Let's take a look…A serious diagnosis forces us to confront the fact that we have an expiration date. In other words, our life span is not infinite. Since we are forced to acknowledge the reality that we will not live forever, we may now view the concept of time as a valuable commodity that shouldn't be wasted. We might stop procrastinating and finish the projects that we began, and have a renewed appreciation of life.

Check off any that you find important.

- ___ Enjoying the moment
- ___ A sense of humor
- ___ Taking better care of yourself
- ___ Learning self-kindness and self-love
- ___ Seeing your life as meaningful
- ___ Being proactive in self-care
- ___ Appreciating the value of the moment
- ___ Being more sensitive to the feelings of others

Which ones do you need to improve upon?

_____
_____
_____
_____

THE GIFT OF PAYING IT FORWARD

How are you using your experiences to help others?

_____
_____
_____
_____

LEARNING TO ACCEPT HELP

Are you comfortable with accepting help and support? _____

Do you have a support system? List any names:

_____
_____
_____
_____

GRATITUDE

Make a Gratitude List (I will help you to begin.)

- Food, clothes, a place to live.
- _____
- _____
- _____
- _____
- _____
- _____
- _____
- _____

CLOSING THOUGHTS

The diagnosis of a serious or a chronic illness is life-changing. Since these illnesses aren't going away, we are forced to grieve, adapt, draw upon our inner strength and courage, and create a new normal that we're comfortable with.

This situation also presents us with a powerful learning opportunity. Nothing will get your attention and force you to evaluate your life more than hearing that you have a chronic or a life-threatening illness. On the plus side, our adversity gives us a unique opportunity to grow personally, and to use our experience and challenges to help others.

14

FORGIVING SEXUAL ASSAULT AND SEXUAL CHILD ABUSE

*I refuse to give you the power over my life anymore.
I release you, and now, I am truly free!*

SEXUAL ASSAULT IS ONE OF THE MOST DIFFICULT OFFENSES TO FORGIVE. Most of the victims are afraid to report the crime because of the humiliation and the way that they are treated by the judicial system. Moreover, they are left with feelings of shame and self-blame. Many victims have PTSD, ongoing nightmares, flashbacks, and a fear of the dark.

Although it is difficult and requires a lot of work, forgiving sexual assault and molestation can be life-changing. It takes the individual on an inner healing journey, from a helpless victim to an empowered survivor. Many of those whom I've spoken with have told me that after they forgave the perpetrator, their lives began to change and improve, and they were able to find peace.

CHILD ABUSE

I think that most would agree that there are few crimes more reprehensible than child sexual abuse. This is why molestation, particularly incest, are the most difficult offenses to forgive. Since parents are supposed to keep their children safe from danger, when parent-child incest occurs, both parents are blamed, because one was the perpetrator and the other one didn't protect their child. Moreover, this violation can result in post-traumatic stress disorder, panic attacks, depression, anxiety, self-blame, shame, and guilt.

The path to healing includes grieving the loss of a happy and safe childhood, forgiving, and closing the door on sad yesterdays. Keep in mind that your forgiveness is a gift to *yourself*.

GRIEF

In order to heal from child sexual abuse, we must go through the grief process, which includes denial, guilt, anger and bargaining, depression and reflection, acceptance, and healing. I was molested when I was a child, which resulted in many years of post-traumatic stress disorder (PTSD). Although recovery work was difficult, it helped me to heal, and support groups were an important part of the healing process. In these groups, you will receive validation, understanding, and compassion among those who have had similar experiences.

If you have been a victim of child sexual abuse, please know that you are not alone. I know your pain because I have lived it. I have also transcended the pain and trauma, and grew stronger. So can you.

Here are some important points to remember:

- It was not your fault, regardless of the circumstances.
- You are forgiving your assailant as a gift to *yourself*.
- Forgiveness will help to heal *your* heart.

RECOVERY STEPS

As you answer the following questions, please take your time, and give yourself permission to feel all your emotions. If you feel uncomfortable, you don't need write the details regarding the actual assault. However, if you feel the need, please do so here.

_____
_____
_____

Did you know the individual? _____

If yes, what was your relationship with this individual?

_____
_____
_____

As best you can, please try to share what you currently feel when you think about this violation.

_____
_____
_____
_____

In what ways has this negatively impacted upon your life?

In what ways has this offense created ongoing issues?

How has it affected your relationship with yourself?

In what ways has it affected your relationships with others?

If your assailant was a family member, describe your current relationship, if any.

_____

_____

_____

Do you feel that you must receive an apology before you can forgive them? _____

Share any additional thoughts and feelings concerning this individual.

_____

_____

_____

_____

_____

_____

STEP 4: WRITE A LETTER

This step involves writing a letter (not to be mailed) to the perpetrator.

Use your answers to the previous questions to assist you in composing this letter. When you have finished, set the letter on fire, and toss the ashes outdoors. This ritual will put you in control and is a powerful gesture of letting go.

CLOSING THOUGHTS

It is difficult to forgive sexual violations, and this is especially true of child molestation. There are painful memories and emotions that might haunt us until we re-visit them and conquer them. When we do so, often our fears and nightmares will gradually melt away.

If you have been victimized, please know that you are not alone, and you are a *survivor*. You no longer need the carry the burden of someone else's crime. You have the right to live your best life and let go of this baggage.

Forgiveness does not mean releasing the perpetrator from responsibility. It means releasing yourself from the emotional connection with this individual, because your pain ties the both of you together. It is saying: "I refuse to give you power over my life anymore. I release you, and now, *I am truly free!*"

15

COMMUNICATION CONTAMINATION

Communication is complicated!

CAN YOU IMAGINE HOW MANY RESENTMENTS COULD BE AVOIDED if we communicated more effectively? In this chapter, we will explore different aspects of communication, including biases, word choices, information processing, and nonverbal clues.

Although we would prefer to believe that we aren't judgmental, in reality, each one of us have learned to be biased through socialization. These biases can create difficulties in our interactions with one another.

GENDER BIASES

The way in which women and men are treated vary according to culture, and unfortunately, gender biases are not yet behind us. In many cultures, women are still held to different standards than men, and the same personality traits are viewed differently depending upon one's gender. For example, assertive men might be viewed as leaders, while assertive women might be seen as demanding, or, (wait for it) not lady-like. (I'm joking—kind of.) Surely, there are still some men who are threatened by strong women, and describe these women by using the B-word or "a nasty woman.". As much I hate to admit this, there are some women who do so as well.

Are you aware of any gender biases that you might have? If yes, jot these down.

_____
_____
_____
_____
_____

CONFIRMATION BIASES

In a confirmation bias, we will tend to remember information that supports our beliefs, while forgetting, misinterpreting, or distorting information that we disagree with. This bias is particularly noticeable in political or religious conversations.

Write down an example where you might have distorted the facts, because you disliked a person, or simply their views.

_____

_____

_____

_____

THE EGOCENTRIC AND THE SELF-SERVING BIASES

These biases occur when we favor a point of view that boosts our self-esteem and credits us for positive events. We might also embellish memories or stories that make us look good. Who hasn't done this? We all would like to be seen as heroes.

Can you give any examples?

_____

_____

_____

_____

_____

_____

ROSY RETROSPECTION

The older we get, the more likely we will be to engage in this bias. When we begin a sentence with "back in the day" or "the good old days," we're engaging in *rosy retrospection*. Here's an example: "*Back in the day*, the movies and music were much better."

Can you share some of your own euphoric memories from "the good old days?"

_____

_____

_____
_____
_____
_____

THE MISINFORMATION EFFECT

This happens when we second-guess ourselves after hearing different interpretations of an event that we've witnessed. These influences might cause us to rethink our own recollections.

Can you give an example of when you have second-guessed yourself?

_____
_____
_____
_____
_____

BODY LANGUAGE

Multiple studies have determined that most communication is non-verbal, and body language can be more persuasive than words. If we're conversing, and I say "I agree with you," while shaking my head from left to right, indicating "no," would you believe my words or my body language? _____.

POSTURE

If I'm speaking to you, and my arms and legs are crossed, how would you interpret this?

_____
_____
_____

What is the first thought you have when you see these gestures? Jot down your answers.

- Slouching _____
- Avoiding eye contact _____

- Smiling _____
- Eye-rolling _____
- Winking _____
- Sighing _____
- Yawning _____

If someone responds to you with any of these gestures, can your interpretation cause you to develop a resentment? _____.

PHYSICAL SPACE (PROXEMICS)

When we interact with others, we feel most comfortable when there is a certain amount of physical distance between us. The four zones of proximity are intimate, personal, social, and public. Generally speaking, most people are not comfortable when someone is within their personal space (1.5 to 2.5 feet), unless they have an intimate relationship with that individual.

Have you ever felt uncomfortable when someone stood too close to you? _____

APPEARANCE

First impressions are powerful, and most of us judge others according to their appearance and how they present themselves. Next to the following descriptions, write down the first thoughts that come to your mind.

A well-dressed man wearing a suit and tie.

_____
_____
_____

An elderly, disheveled woman pushing a shopping cart.

_____
_____
_____

A man who is stumbling and slurring.

_____

A woman with her hair in a bun and wearing eyeglasses.

_____

_____

_____

And unshaven man with dirty hands and fingernails.

_____

_____

_____

PARALANGUAGE

Paralanguage is the way in which we say our words. This includes our accents, the pitch of our voice, and how loudly or softly we speak.

ACCENTS

There is a lot of bias concerning regional or foreign accents. When my grandparents came to America, they were mocked because of their Italian accents. Even within the USA, individuals are judged according to their regional accents. For example, those with strong southern or New York accents.

Have you ever found yourself making presumptions based upon someone's accent? _____

Have you ever been judged because of your accent? _____

If yes, in what ways?

_____

_____

_____

_____

VOICE VOLUME

There are many misinterpretations which are based upon how loudly or how softly people speak. In the United States, loud voices are usually interpreted as angry or rude. However, in some cultures, an increase in voice volume might be socially acceptable.

What is your first thought in the following scenarios?

A man speaking loudly: _____

A man whispering: _____

A woman speaking loudly: _____

A woman whispering: _____

Were your interpretations different for men and women? _____

PARA-VERBAL COMMUNICATION

Para-verbal messages are interpreted according to the words that we emphasize. Here's an interesting example. Think about the sentence, "I owe you an apology." It seems straightforward, doesn't it? Now, read it aloud, emphasizing the different words in italics:

"*I* owe you an apology."

"I owe *you* an apology."

"I owe you an *apology*."

Can you see how the emphasized word completely changes the meaning of the sentence? _____

CLOSING THOUGHTS

As you can see, communication is complicated! There are layers upon layers of variables, including biases, voice volume, physical appearance, foreign and regional accents, body language, and so much more. Because of this, even a simple conversation can be confusing and riddled with misinterpretations.

If we are more aware of these complexities, it will help us interact with others, and eliminate some of the communication contamination which can lead to resentments.

16

ESTABLISHING HEALTHY BOUNDARIES

*Many misunderstandings, conflicts, and resentments
can be avoided with clear boundaries.*

We all have physical and emotional boundaries that communicate to others what we find acceptable and comfortable in our interactions. Our physical boundaries include our personal space and our privacy. An intrusion into our physical boundaries can include unwelcome touches, someone standing too close to us (intruding upon our personal space), or any invasions of our privacy. Emotional boundaries involve our feelings and our reactions to particular words, comments, and situations.

Most of us find it difficult to set boundaries because we really haven't been taught how to do so. What do we say? How do we say it? In this chapter we will work on ways to assertively (not aggressively) express our discomfort when our boundaries have been violated.

WHAT ARE OUR BOUNDARIES?

Before we can establish boundaries, we need to consider what we find offensive. Answering these questions will help you to determine your personal boundaries.

What makes you angry?

_____

_____

_____

What feels like disrespect?

_____

_____

_____

What makes you feel that someone has taken advantage of you?

_____

_____

_____

Are there particular words that you find offensive? List below.

_____

_____

_____

Are there certain behaviors that make you feel uncomfortable? List below.

_____

_____

_____

Assertion Versus Aggression

If one of our boundaries has been violated, we need to express this in an assertive, but calm way. If others don't feel that they are being attacked, then they will be less inclined to take offense. Keep in mind that people can violate our boundaries without realizing this. If you politely share your discomfort, and the offending person becomes defensive, you can exit the conversation and say: "I don't feel that we're getting anywhere, so we can discuss this at another time." If the individual is being defensive, then they aren't open to hearing what you're trying to share.

The way in which we assert our discomfort will vary according to the type of relationship we have with particular individuals. For example, your choice of words would be different in a personal relationship than it would be in a professional relationship. Sometimes we can be in a difficult position if our employer is the person who is violating our boundaries. In this case, we need to weigh the pros and cons of asserting our boundaries versus letting it go.

Give two examples of how you would assert your boundaries in a personal relationship.

_____

_____

_____

Give two examples of how you would assert your boundaries with a peer at work.

_____

_____

_____

Write down two examples of how you would assert your boundaries with supervisors.

_____

_____

DELICATE SITUATIONS

There's an old saying which states that when you marry someone, you also marry their family. This also applies to life partners. In these situations, we need to be more subtle and diplomatic in asserting ourselves. The sentence, "I'm sorry you feel this way," is a good and gentle response to in-laws or our extended family.

CLOSING THOUGHTS

If someone disrespects our boundaries, we should *assertively* tell that person that we are offended by their comments or behavior. If we don't, there's a possibility that it will happen again. Most people will respect our boundaries if we share our feelings and discomfort in a respectful manner, and without assigning blame. As we continue to assert ourselves, we will begin to feel more comfortable in doing so. More importantly, this will help us to avoid miscommunication that can often lead to resentments. Practice makes better.

17

RELEASING TOXIC RELATIONSHIPS

*In leaving toxic relationships, you are taking
a monumental step toward self-love and self-respect.*

PEOPLE COME AND GO IN OUR LIVES, either by choice or due to circumstances. Still, every person we meet is there for a purpose, and we learn lessons from each individual who crosses our path. However, some friendships and relationships can become toxic over time. And then, we might find that we're asking ourselves, "How did I get here?"

Conflicts might begin to escalate and remain unresolved. The other individual might be resistant to healthy conflict resolution. We might have reached a point where we regret investing any more time in the relationship. We might feel unappreciated, scapegoated, or abused. We may feel drained, weary, and tired of being a part of someone else's constant tornado, where the relationship feels like a series of ongoing, endless battles.

And so, at this point, we are at a crossroads. We need to make hard choices.

Is it worth losing our self-respect to remain in a toxic and painful situation? Do we choose ongoing pain and endless trauma-drama, or do we choose self-love?

And then, perhaps after prayer for guidance and strength, we might select the healthier choice—self-respect. Cognizant of the consequences, and realizing that we will probably grieve the losses, we bravely release the toxic relationship, and take with us the learning lessons, detaching with forgiveness, not resentment.

Most relationships begin positively. If we didn't like something about the person, we wouldn't have pursued a relationship. Of course, concerning family, this becomes more complicated, because, let's face it, we didn't choose them. They're connected to us by circumstances, shared history, and memories. At the same time, if they're toxic, it's more difficult to sever ties, because of our histories and the above-mentioned memories. (As they say, "you can choose your friends, but not your relatives.")

However, in terms of friends and love interests, initially, there was something about this individual which attracted us. Gradually, the dynamics might begin to change and morph into toxicity. Conflicts might arise and remain unresolved. We might lose trust in this individual, or we regret investing time in the relationship.

Can you list relationships which began on a positive note, but later became filled with negativity or conflict?

_____

_____

_____

_____

_____

Can you identify any toxic warning signs?

_____

_____

_____

_____

If you found yourself in a relationship that turned sour, how did you address this situation? Check off all that apply.

_____ Directly asked the person why there was a change in the relationship.

_____ Discussed and resolved the conflict.

_____ Ignored the situation, hoping it would go away.

_____ Reduced contact with the person.

_____ Stopped all contact with that person.

_____ Became angry and harbored a resentment.

_____ Argued.

_____ Spread gossip about that person to gather allies.

_____ Sought revenge.

_____ Assumed the victim role.

_____ Used tears to gain sympathy.

WHERE IT ALL BEGAN: SOURCES AND ORIGINS

What did you learn about relationships from your parents?

_____
_____
_____
_____

How did your parents respond to offenses? Circle all that apply.

- Angry
- Vengeful
- Embarrassed
- Forgiving
- Understanding
- Hateful
- Jealous
- Unforgiving
- Others: _____

Do you see where you might have adopted any of these sentiments? If so, which ones?

_____
_____

What did you learn about relationships from watching television?

_____
_____

List particular TV shows or movies that influenced your views about relationships when you were growing up:

_____
_____
_____

_____

_____

Do you think that your family-of-origin and the influences of television might have affected your beliefs concerning relationships? _____.

SIGNS OF TOXIC RELATIONSHIPS

In a healthy relationship, there are times to speak and times to listen. There should also be a spirit of mutual support. At times, the balance might shift, where one person might need more support than the other, but the shift should then flow back to a give-and-take balance.

Do one or more of your relationships feel one-sided? _____

If so, list the names.

_____

_____

_____

_____

Are these individuals unreasonable and deflective? _____

Is there unnecessary drama, arguments, or conflicts in the relationship? _____

Do small disagreements explode into huge issues? _____

Is the person unwilling to have an honest conversation? _____

Does it feel like you're doing all the giving, while the other individual is doing all of the taking? _____

Let's take closer look ...

BLAMING AND DEFLECTING

The Buddha said that when we point a finger at someone, the other three fingers are pointing back at us. Jesus taught that before we look at the speck in the other person's eye, first we need to address the plank in our own eye. Assigning blame to others will never resolve a conflict, but it does have the ability create further damage.

Let's look at some common toxic relationship responses.

What is the level of toxicity in the relationship?

If you are willing to explore the level of dysfunction in a particular relationship, then you might have an opportunity to change it.

Take this short **quiz** to determine how toxic the relationship is. Rate each answer from 1 to 5, by using the following scale.

Never—1
Occasionally—2
A little too much—3
Frequently —4
Always—5

1) When you have a conflict, do either of you blame the other or seek retaliation? _____

2) Do either of you respond with threats? _____

3) Do either of you insist upon being right? _____

4) Do either of you hold grudges for extended periods of time? _____

5) Are either of you manipulative or controlling? _____

6) Do either of you gossip, embellish the truth, or lie to get sympathy? _____

7) Do either of you betray confidentiality when you're angry? _____

8) Does this happen frequently? _____

9) Do either of you disrespect or ignore boundaries? _____

10) Are either of you combative? _____

<u>Add up your scores.</u>

1-10 — Your relationship is fairly healthy.
11-20 — There are some dysfunctional qualities in the relationship.
21-30 — The danger zone.
31-40 — The relationship is toxic.
41-50 — If the interactions don't change, the relationship should and will end.

RECONCILIATION OR RELEASE?

Ideally, we should try our best to have an honest conversation with our friend or romantic interest, and attempt to work things out. If we can't, then reconciliation doesn't need to be a part of the forgiveness process. We can forgive and let go of our hurt, and still leave the relationship if there's no hope for a solution. If someone continues to overstep, then we must carefully consider whether or not this relationship is worth investing more of our time and energy. There are times when the only option is to walk away from an unhealthy relationship. In severing ties with unhealthy people, we are taking away their power to create further disruption in our lives. Nevertheless, it is important to exit these situations with forgiveness, so we are free from lingering resentments.

ENERGY VAMPIRES—A PARTICULAR BRAND OF TOXICITY

What are energy vampires? How do we recognize them? How do we deal with them?

Whenever we communicate with another person we are exchanging energy. There are some people, however, that can drain our energy, and they're called *energy vampires*. These people are usually attracted to ongoing conflict. When one source of conflict ends, they feel compelled to initiate another. Let's delve a bit further…

Have you ever been around a person where you experienced a sense of well-being and comfort, even if you weren't well acquainted—You simply felt their good vibes? _____

In contrast, have you ever had this thought? "I don't know what it is about this person, but I feel very uncomfortable around them. I'm getting an uncomfortable feeling, or picking up negative energy." _____

There are certain *vibes* that we pick up from different people that can be difficult to explain. Some people might describe a particular person with amazing positive energy, using the cliché: "That person lights up a room." However, it has nothing to do with how they look, how they speak, or what they say. It is related to the *energy* that this individual projects out into the world.

However, when we're interacting with an *energy vampire,* the opposite is true. We can actually feel our own energy being depleted when we're around this person. We might even feel emotional or physical discomfort. Energy is powerful.

Identifying the Energy Vampires in Your Life

Do your interactions with a particular person seem to drain your energy? _____

Do you feel weary or tired after talking to this individual? _____

Does your mood change?

_____

Do you dread the thought of being around this person?

_____

Certain individuals with particular personality traits are more likely to be energy vampires, and they come in all shapes and sizes. Here are some examples:

If the individual has narcissistic tendencies, and is self-absorbed, then even a brief conversation with them can deplete your energy. They simply cannot stop talking about themselves.

Other energy vampires live their lives as perpetual victims or martyrs, they usually believe that they have bad luck and they're being victimized by everyone around them. They will become angry if you offer them a solution to their problems, because they find comfort in remaining a martyr.

Some energy vampires are passive-aggressive. These individuals will gossip about you, but will not confront you directly. Others might be overtly aggressive and consistently angry, and might target you as their scapegoat. This allows them to divert the blame and avoid taking responsibility.

And finally, we have the crisis-oriented energy vampire. This person is a drama king or queen, who creates one crisis after another at everyone else's expense. After a while, others will get tired of this exhausting, ongoing drama.

With drama vampires, the last question you should ask is, "How are you?" because they are never well, and they will be more than happy to tell you why. They also think that their problem is much worse than anyone else's and is unsolvable. They crave negative attention.

Years ago, I had an acquaintance who was always suffering about one thing or another. If you asked her, "How are you," her usual response was, "I'm dying." Added to this, if you called her voicemail, in her recording, she made a determined effort to sound like she really was "dying."

Protecting Ourselves

None of us enter a friendship or an intimate relationship with the idea that some day, it will need to end. However, sometimes relationships change and become more negative than positive, and then we must evaluate our options.

Valid Reasons to Consider Exiting a Relationship

1. If the relationship has more suffering than happiness.
2. If the other individual is abusive.
3. If the relationship is based upon manipulation.
4. If the individual is unpredictable.
5. If the relationship causes ongoing anxiety.
6. If the person is judgmental or overly critical.
7. If you feel that you need to constantly defend yourself.
8. If the relationship creates chaos in your life.
9. If you only hear from that person when they want something from you.
10. If the other individual is a taker, but never gives.
11. If the relationship is only about borrowing or lending money.
12. If you are being used as a scapegoat.
13. If the other person has an unresolved resentment toward you.
14. If the individual becomes angry whenever you disagree with them.
15. If your shared philosophy changes.
16. If he/she isn't making an effort to compromise.
17. If ongoing issues are not resolved.
18. If the relationship lack mutual support.

CLOSING THOUGHTS

When we have a relationship conflict, we need to take a step back and ask ourselves, "What can I learn from this situation?" Conflicts can be learning opportunities, and dysfunctional relationships can be healed under certain circumstances. Each individual must be willing to assume responsibility for their part in the dysfunction, listen to the other person's perspective, assume responsibility and make a commitment to change. Boundaries might also need to be re-established. The possibility of reversing toxicity in a relationship also depends upon the level of the current dysfunction.

If someone has offended you, and you want to respond with the anger—don't. Step away from the situation for now, and take a time-out to explore the dynamics of this particular relationship to consider whether or not you wish to remain in this situation.

Sometimes we stay in unhealthy friendships or relationships because we keep hoping that things will improve, and it can take some time before we can muster up the courage to permanently let go. We need to be ready.

It is nearly impossible to maintain any level of self-respect if we allow ourselves to be continuously disrespected by others. In detaching from toxic relationships that have no hope of healing, we are taking a colossal step toward self-love and self-respect. Now, we can reclaim our lives and rebuild our self-worth.

18

MINDFULNESS, MEDITATION & FORGIVENESS EXERCISES

*Once we begin to discover and embrace our center –
our core of serenity—we will see people and situations differently.*

THE ART & PRACTICE OF MINDFULNESS

When we embrace our resentments, the last place we want to be is in the present moment. We're too busy reliving the offense (the past), and possibly contemplating retaliation (the future). Therefore, it requires a lot of effort to bring our minds back to where our bodies are—right here and right now. When we are able to do so, however, we are able to calm our thoughts and see situations with enhanced clarity, good judgment, and wisdom. This is the essence of being mindful.

Confucius is credited as saying, "Wherever you go, there you are." So true! Our reality is shaped by our thoughts. If we're in the present moment, then we're not thinking about yesterday or tomorrow. This is exactly where we need to be! Mindfulness is the practice that helps us to be consciously aware of everything in the present moment. Let's have some fun and do an experiment. I would like you turn your focus outward and observe your surroundings through the senses of hearing, seeing, smelling, and touching.

Right now, what sounds do you hear?

_____

_____

_____

Right now, what sights do you see?

_____

_____

_____

Do you notice anything that you weren't aware of before?

_____
_____
_____
_____

Right now, what scents do you smell?

_____
_____

Touch an object in the room. What does it feel like?

_____
_____

Were you unaware of these senses a minute ago, before I brought them to your attention? _____.

In general, are you experiencing them in more detail than usual? _____

This moment-to-moment, enhanced awareness is mindfulness. It allows us to experience life to its fullest and also enhances our relationships and our communication with others.

You will probably find that mindfulness has a calming effect, and will help you to take control of your racing thoughts. It will also help to lower your blood pressure, relieve anxiety, and, more importantly, help you to appreciate the present moment. When we think about the past, although we might periodically recall pleasant memories, most of the time, our thoughts are negative. When we think about the future, often our thoughts are fear-based or catastrophic. These backward and forward focuses have us living a constant state of stress and fear.

We cannot change what happened yesterday and we don't have control over what might happen tomorrow. We only own this moment, and can control how we approach today. How we choose to live today will influence our tomorrow.

Here's another enlightening exercise. Monitor your thoughts for one day, and at the conclusion of the day, answer these questions.

How many minutes (or hours) did you spend thinking about the past? _____.

How many of those minutes (or hours) were spent on negative thoughts? _____.

How many minutes (or hours) did you spend thinking about the future? _____.

How many of those minutes (or hours) were spent on negative thoughts? _____.

When I do this exercise with clients, they're surprised by the amount of time their mind spends living in the past and the future, and how most of their thoughts were negative.

Were you surprised, too? _____.

Our attitudes play a crucial role in the practice and the success of mindfulness. Let's look at these helpful mindsets:

- Avoiding judgment.
- Cultivating patience.
- Trying to view the world with a childlike wonder and innocence.
- Trusting your intuition and wisdom.
- Going with the flow of life (non-resistance).
- Avoiding anxiety over taking the next step.
- Trying to fully be in the moment.
- Accepting what you can't change, and changing what you can.
- Letting go of your lingering feelings concerning situations beyond your control.

List the attitudes you have that you can currently identify:

_____
_____
_____
_____
_____

Give real-life examples of how you have demonstrated each mindset:

Avoiding judgment.

_____
_____
_____
_____

Having patience.

___

Observing a situation with a childlike wonder.

___

Trusting in yourself, honoring your feelings, intuition and wisdom.

___

Going with the flow.

___

Accepting what you can't change, and changing what you can.

___

Letting go and moving forward.

_____
_____
_____
_____

Jot down the mindsets that you plan to work on.

_____
_____
_____
_____

THE FLOWER-PHOTO FORGIVENESS RITUAL

If you are having a particularly difficult time forgiving someone on your list, then this ritual might be helpful to you. You will need a vase with a flower, and a photo of the person. If a photo is unavailable, envision a picture of the person near the vase. (The flower can be real or artificial.)

Each day for 30 days, look at the photo (or envision the person). Then tell that person aloud that you would like them to have all of the good things in life that you want for yourself. (This may be difficult at the beginning, but it gets easier each day.)

Sample Script:

"Hi, (person's name). Today I am sending you compassion and light. I wish you health, happiness, prosperity, and serenity. May all of your dreams come true."

At the end of the 30 days, write down how you feel:

_____
_____
_____

Did your feelings towards this individual change? _____. If yes, explain.

Did the resentment melt away? _____.

MEDITATION

Meditation differs from mindfulness in a couple of ways. When we meditate, we set aside a specific amount of time at a specific hour each day. We need to stop our other activities, and sit in a quiet environment alone, without interruption. In contrast, the practice of mindfulness is included in our daily activities. Both practices involve focusing upon the present moment. In meditation, we focus on a mantra. The mantra, is repeated in a rhythmic fashion. Many people use the word "Om" as their mantra. As our thoughts float through our mind, we continue to bring back our focus to the present moment by repeating our mantra. Gradually, our random thoughts will lessen. Try to be patient with yourself. It takes time to evolve in meditation. Practice makes better.

CLOSING THOUGHTS

In closing this chapter, I am going to share two guided meditations with you. The first one will help you to relax, while the second one will help you with self-love, self-esteem, and self-forgiveness. After a while, you will be able to memorize the words, and repeat them in your mind with your eyes closed. (There are additional meditations in my book, *The Forgiveness Journey*.) Please find a quiet place where you can sit comfortably without being disturbed.

GUIDED RELAXATION MEDITATION

Allow yourself to relax, as you sense a peaceful feeling extend throughout your entire body, from your head to your toes.

Now, feel the muscles relaxing around your forehead.

Feel your neck, your chest,p, and your arms melting into relaxation.

Now, feel your stomach muscles relaxing, your thighs and legs gradually following.

Become aware of the tingling in your toes as they begin to relax.

Once you are lulled into a state of full relaxation and calm, think back to a happy moment that you can recall. It might something as simple as looking at a beautiful butterfly, or sitting on a beach.

Maybe it was a song that filled your heart with joy.

Allow this memory to create a sense of warmth and serenity within you.

SELF-LOVE MEDITATION

As you relax, gently become aware of your thoughts. Notice if any of your thoughts are judgmental. Recognize how interesting it is to see your mind at work.

Feel compassion toward yourself.

Did you notice many self-critical thoughts? Know that we all have these, and you are not alone.

Say, "I love you," to yourself.

Envision someone or something that brings joy to your heart.

It could be a person or an animal companion. It could be an activity that you enjoy.

Repeat these kind words to yourself:

May you feel safe and protected... May you be joyful and peaceful...

May you be healthy and strong... May you find inner peace...

May you learn how to love and accept yourself exactly as you are...

Envision yourself inhaling these kind words. Exhale any tension.

Relax...

19

OBSTACLE BUSTERS

These ceremonies will help you to replenish your soul.

OBSTACLE BUSTERS ARE EXERCISES THAT HELP US TO COUNTERACT the negative feelings we have about ourselves.

DAILY SELF-ESTEEM EXERCISE

Look in a mirror. What is your first thought? Jot it down here before you forget it. Our thoughts move by quickly.

_____

_____

I asked five men and five women this question, and here were the responses:

- "I hate mirrors."
- "I see too many wrinkles."
- "I look pale"
- "I need more makeup."
- "Damn, I'm getting old."
- "I need to lose some weight."
- "I'm starting to lose my hair."
- "I wish that I was more attractive."
- "I notice more grays."
- "My face looks puffy."

Not one person had a positive thought about themselves!

We all have the tendency to be overly self-critical yet find it difficult to recognize our good qualities. Therefore, we need to replace these self-defeating messages with more positive ones. Since we aren't accustomed to saying kind words to ourselves, this may feel strange at the beginning. When have you ever said "I love you" to yourself?

I'm guessing never. As you continue to say these affirmations, you will become less self-critical and more aware of your positive qualities. One day, you'll look in the mirror and notice that your first thought is *not negative*! The first exercise is to be done in the morning, and the second before you go to sleep.

MORNING EXERCISE

Look in the mirror and say to yourself (out loud):

"Good morning. I love you.

You're looking good today!

I'm grateful for this new day.

I have a choice to make it a good day.

I will take responsibility for all of my decisions.

I forgive you for any mistakes you might make.

I still love you."

EVENING EXERCISE

Look in the mirror and say to yourself (out loud):

"Good evening. I love you.

I'm sorry for any mistakes that I have made today.

I will learn from them, and do better tomorrow.

I forgive you.

I still love you."

THE SELF-FORGIVENESS EXERCISE/RITUAL

As we continue to criticize ourselves through the years, this diminishes our confidence and our ability to like ourselves. This two-step exercise will help you to change your perspective.

Step #1

Picture yourself as a 6 year-old child. Envision looking into the eyes of your younger self. Do you see the younger you as lovable? Keep in mind that you are still you, only older. You were lovable and worthy of love then, and you still are.

Say to yourself, "I'm still lovable."

Now allow yourself to feel this inner child's unconditional love for you. Feel this love flowing through you.

What are your first thoughts and feelings?

_____
_____

What was it like to look into your younger eyes, bringing forth your inner child?

_____
_____
_____
_____

Step #2

At some point during your day, look in the mirror again and do this exercise. Say these words out loud:

"I am not my self-criticisms. I am far more than my faults and fears. I'm here for a reason and a greater purpose. I am here to learn and teach. *I am the beautiful soul in the mirror.*"

Try to embrace this truth.

Write down three positive qualities that you like about yourself.

1. _____.
2. _____.
3. _____.

CLOSING THOUGHTS

Each day we are presented with endless possibilities and choices. That's the great thing about life. If we're having a difficult day, we can start our day over again. If need be, we can also start our life over again!

- Encourage yourself.
- Be kind to yourself.
- Forgive yourself.
- Be your best *you* for today.
- Then repeat tomorrow.

In time, these ceremonies will help you to feel genuine self-love, replenish your soul, and assist you in moving forward in your forgiveness journey. They have been helpful to myself and countless others, and I hope that they resonate with you as well. After we forgive ourselves for being imperfect, we need to carry this message to others—leading by example. We need to strive toward loving ourselves like our animal companions love us. Now, that's a whole lot of love!

20

SEEKING FORGIVENESS FROM OTHERS

The ability to make amends is a huge leap in personal growth.

EVEN THOUGH WE WOULD LIKE AN APOLOGY WHEN WE HAVE BEEN OFFENDED, often it can be difficult to admit that we might have offended others, and an apology is in order on our end. This chapter will explore situations where you were the offender rather than the offended, possibly causing others to hold resentments toward you.

There are going to be times when we offend other people. Although it might be unintentional, this doesn't erase the damage. Depending upon the circumstances, we might owe someone else an apology, and possibly monetary restitution. The work in this chapter will help you to develop an attitude of self-reflection and accountability, so you can recognize and rectify your mistakes quickly.

It's not always easy to look at ourselves and acknowledge our errors or lapses in judgment. The role of the offender is not endearing. Nevertheless, rectifying our errors has its own rewards and can be an opportunity for personal growth. We can make our amends with dignity and grace, and learn from our mistakes. We all have character flaws and, unfortunately, sometimes our behavior can harm others. Our task is to learn from and correct our mistakes, and the first step is to acknowledge them.

LET'S TAKE A QUICK INVENTORY.

Do you insist upon getting the last word in an argument? _____

Do you feel inadequate if you don't win an argument? _____

When you are angry, is it difficult to control your temper and your words? _____

Is it important to you to be right in every situation? _____

To acknowledge our mistakes, we need to put aside our egos and be honest with ourselves. Unless we accept responsibility, nothing will change. This simple admission creates the path forward toward personal growth. Like forgiveness, choosing to correct and rectify our errors is a conscious decision.

In the role of the offender, can you see how difficult it can be to apologize? It requires humility to recognize our errors and rectify them. However, doing so is very healing and freeing. Let's get started.

List the name(s) of those whom you have offended and owe an apology, as well as the offense.

_____

_____

_____

MAKING AMENDS

In twelve-step groups, there is great emphasis upon forgiving others as well as making amends and restitution for our own offenses. An amend should be specific to individual circumstances. Essentially, it is about compensating an offended individual with what was lost as a result of the offense. In some cases, it might include monetary compensation.

ALTERNATIVE SOLUTIONS

There are some situations where direct amends aren't possible. Perhaps the individual is deceased or inaccessible. Then you can make restitution indirectly by making a donation in their honor or memory.

It isn't always easy to apologize. In fact, sometimes it is just as difficult to apologize as it is to forgive certain people. Try to see this from the other person's perspective. By apologizing, you are giving this individual an opportunity to forgive you. This exchange can heal both of you.

Even if the individual is unable to accept your apology, you will find that this won't damper the relief that you experience. Like forgiveness, the ability to make amends is a huge leap in personal growth. This opportunity takes us to the next level, since we are following through with our commitment to making things right.

CHOOSING THE RIGHT WORDS

Ownership and proper wording are vital when we are seeking forgiveness from others. Some apologies are ambiguous, and they are designed to avoid taking responsibility. If you want to irritate the offended person and make a bad situation worse, here are a few gems:

- "I'm sorry that *you* were offended"
- "I'm sorry that *you* feel that way."
- "I'm sorry *you* misunderstood me."
- "I'm sorry that *you misinterpreted* my words or intentions."

These words might seem like apologies, but they actually place the responsibility of the offense on the offended, rather than the offender. They lack ownership. In these examples, you are blaming the other person for reacting poorly to *your* offense. Not nice! If you are truly seeking forgiveness, then your apology needs to contain some essential components.

A compelling apology must contain these elements:

1. You understand and acknowledge *your* misdeed.
2. You know *why* it was hurtful, inappropriate, and wrong.
3. You feel regret and remorse.
4. *You* take responsibility for *your* inappropriate or hurtful behavior.
5. You promise not to repeat the offense.

Don't blame the victim! There is a huge difference between saying, "I'm sorry that *your* feelings were hurt," and, "I'm sorry that *I* hurt your feelings." A good apology starts with, "I'm sorry that I said or did _____," or, "Please forgive me for _____."

When you validate the offended person's feelings and express remorse, most individuals will accept your apology. The words, "I'm sorry," are healing. The words, "Please forgive me," are empowering *as well as* healing. It is difficult to remain angry, when someone humbly asks for forgiveness.

What if the person refuses to accept your apology? This can happen. Just as we struggle to forgive some people and offenses, so do others. If the individual does not want to accept your apology, you have still done your part. You will need to accept their decision and move on.

If someone is not ready to forgive you, there's nothing you can say that will change their mind. Maybe they will feel differently in the future. Walk away with grace and integrity, knowing that you have done everything possible to rectify your error.

ONGOING ACCOUNTABILITY

By making restitution quickly, you will avoid an accumulation of baggage that gets heavier as time goes on. Immediately rectifying your mistakes will keep your life on a healthy forward path, free of debris and unnecessary headaches.

CLOSING THOUGHTS

In this chapter, we have come full circle on the topic of forgiveness. Since we know that it's not always easy to forgive someone, we can understand that others might feel this way toward us. Keep this in mind if someone cannot find it in their heart to forgive you right now.

If the individual accepts your apology, that's a gift. If the person is unable to do so right now, you can still walk away with renewed self-respect, knowing that you've done the honorable thing. Either way, be gracious.

21

BONUS CHAPTER: LIVING PROACTIVELY

Offense is better than defense.

IN SPORTS, THERE IS A POPULAR SLOGAN WHICH READS: "the best defense is a good offense."

This philosophy also applies to the art of living proactively. If we approach life from this perspective, we can avoid some of the inevitable *potholes* in life, and use our previous experiences to address similar situations that might come up in the future.

It isn't uncommon to repeat the same mistakes, even when we know that the outcome wasn't favorable in the past. Why is it that we keep falling into the same potholes over and over again? We are living from a defensive position and we're not using our life experiences to address similar situations in the future.

The first time we make a mistake, we might have received an outcome that we didn't expect. That's understandable. This experience should teach us that our actions brought about negative consequences. But… does it? Not always.

Sometimes, despite our best efforts, we can easily default to familiar, self-defeating pattern of behavior. As we keep falling into the same metaphorical *potholes*, we are going to get weary after a while. Come on! How many times can we say "oops" without getting annoyed with ourselves? Life teaches us valuable lessons. However, our lessons are only *valuable* if use them to our benefit in the future. This is when these metaphorical *holes* have the power to create *wholeness*.

A large part of living proactively is the ability to foresee and avoid the same mistakes. We need to use our past experiences to help us in making proactive decisions in upcoming similar situations. When we're in a proactive frame-of-mind, we respond rather than react. This is self-empowerment.

Here are some proactive steps:

1. I make a mistake, and the outcome was to my detriment.
2. Good grief, I did it again. I acted without thinking. It was a reflex response.

3. I'm getting tired of making the same mistakes.
4. I am now able to pause, remember past experiences, think it through, and make a more informed decision.
5. Whew!

Can you share an example where you applied one or all of these proactive steps in your life?

_____

_____

_____

The Delicate Art of Declining Requests

- Are you tired of saying "yes", when you really want to say "no?" _____
- Do you feel taken advantage of? _____
- Do you resent the fact that you are seen as the "go to" person? _____
- Do you get angry with yourself for saying yes when you really want to say no? _____

If you can say *yes* to any of these questions, then you are probably approaching life from a defensive, rather than an offensive position. You are living reactively rather than proactively. In this position, you are reacting to the events in life, rather than thinking them through, and then, responding to them.

Here are a few typical comments from those who might approach life from a defensive position:

In response to a request for help:

"Okay. I'll help you. No problem." But, you might be thinking, *"Damn it! Why can't I bring myself to say no."*

Or, you might blame the other person, saying to yourself, *"How dare he ask me to help him again!"* (But, are you actually angry with yourself?)

Or, you might think, *"He always has a million excuses when I ask **him** for a favor."*

And so, you might begin to feel like a victim, and develop a resentment toward the imposing person *and* yourself. This can all change when you consciously shift gears to the offensive position in your life.

Where to start...

The word "no" can be difficult to express, since it has a negative connotation attached to it. Moreover, we might cringe at the thought of denying someone's request for help. This is usually because we want to be liked, and we don't want people to become angry or disappointed with us. None of us want to be looked upon as the *bad guys*. In chapter 15, we looked at how our word choices could be perceived and possibly misinterpreted by others. Let's delve into this a bit further...

How can we politely decline a request without using the infamous word "no"?

If we ask someone for a favor or for help, and they respond with the word "no" without further explanation, most of us would take personal offense. This word has been stigmatized, and it sounds blunt and rude.

So, let's test out other options. How about this response: "I'm sorry, but I'm busy, so I can't help you." This response will buy you some time, but does not get you completely off the hook. Some people are persistent and don't take *no* for an answer. This type of individual might respond by saying, "OK, then can you help me tomorrow or next week?"

Do you see the problem? The ball is back on our side of the tennis court. Ok, so that doesn't really work to our benefit.

Let's try again ...

If we decline by category, then this eliminates the feeling of a personal rejection, and closes the door to the possibility that we can help at another time. Allow me to explain... For example, my husband and I have a vehicle that's a truck with an extended cab. I can't tell you how many people have asked us for help in moving furniture or other items. We became the *go-to* people for free hauling, and this had to stop.

Now, if someone asks us to use our truck and help them to move anything, we reply by saying, "I'm sorry, but we don't do that anymore. But I know that you can rent a truck from Home Depot for about $20. Why not give them a call." With this response, we are making this decline impersonal, while offering a solution. So, in the category of helping through the use of our truck, we decline. This tactic can apply to absolutely any other category as well.

THE PAUSE

Often, when we feel uncomfortable, we might immediately say "yes" without giving ourselves the time to decide.

Have you ever had a reflex response when someone asked you for a favor? _____

Did you ever feel angry with yourself because you impulsively agreed to take on burdens you weren't expecting, or didn't want? _____

In pausing, we give ourselves time to think about whether or not we want to oblige, so we don't agree simply because we're uncomfortable.

UNWARRANTED GUILT

Have you ever thought about how much time we waste, when we feel guilty for asserting ourselves, and declining a request? _____

I don't know about you, but, in the past, I could ruminate feeling guilty for hours.

Will you make a commitment now to stop feeling guilty for asserting yourself? _____

We need to applaud ourselves for respecting our priorities and taking charge of our lives, not beating ourselves up. If you're unable to fulfill someone's request, this doesn't make you a bad person. Sometimes we people-please because we don't want to look bad in the eyes of others. Reasonable people, however, will understand that we have our own lives and commitments, and might be unavailable at time.

CLOSING THOUGHTS

Declining requests without guilt is the beginning of living our lives proactively. From there, we will begin to cultivate an attitude of self-assertiveness, which will branch out to other areas in our lives.

It takes some practice to live proactively. In the beginning, it will feel uncomfortable. Don't give up. With time you will experience the indirect consequences of taking this position, and you will feel more empowered and in control of your life. More importantly, so many resentments can be avoided when we proactively assert ourselves.

22

EPILOGUE

What if... every human being was able to forgive?

THE ACT OF FORGIVENESS IS ABOUT LETTING GO OF PAINFUL BAGGAGE, so we can move forward, and live our best lives, unencumbered. This simple act gives us possibilities in our lives that were previously tethered by the consequences of our unresolved resentments.

Forgiveness touches all areas of our lives in one way or another and can be life transforming. It is so much more than a one-to-one encounter, where we are merely releasing one another from debts owed. Rather, the ramifications have a ripple effect.

What if… every human being was able to forgive? Can you imagine how different our world would be? No resentments or grudges—No debris from the past stifling our potential. What would that look like?

Gandhi said that we should be the change that we want to see in the world. It all begins with one person teaching another, and leading by example. Each of us has the capacity to be that person. Our ability to help one another in meaningful ways is profound.

The forgiveness journey never really ends. Just when we think that we've mastered the art of forgiveness, another unexpected situation will confront us and challenge us to forgive yet again. We are consistently reminded that forgiving isn't as easy as we might have remembered it. It takes work. Sometimes it can be a formidable task!

Life always seems to challenge us and push us to grow on deeper levels, even if we're not particularly thrilled to walk the forgiveness path yet again. However, each new opportunity to forgive, affords us the gift of additional wisdom and insight.

Each of us will walk many forgiveness journeys throughout our lives. It's unavoidable. However, the experience and the growth that we've achieved from our former forgiveness journeys will make future journeys much easier. Therefore, the next time that you must forgive someone, (and trust me, you will), the experience and the growth that you've achieved from your former journeys will make that next journey much easier. If we truly invest in our personal growth and do the work, we will be reborn in increments and become a better version of who we once were. It's ongoing. It's challenging. Sometimes it's even painful. But, it's worth it! If I could leave you with one message, it would be to use your knowledge and experiences with forgiveness to help someone else. Pay it forward. Help others to heal their hearts. Then maybe, someday, the *what-if's* mentioned at the beginning of this epilogue can become a reality. The torch is now in your hands.

I wish you healing and transformation in your own journey.

Sending you serenity, love, and light,

Nella

DID YOU LIKE THE FORGIVENESS JOURNEY WORKBOOK?

I would like to take a moment to thank you for reading *The Forgiveness Journey Workbook*. It means a lot to me. If you liked this book, would you be kind enough to let others know? I would really appreciate it.

You can do so by:

- Leaving a brief review on Amazon and Barnes & Noble.
- Leaving a review on Goodreads.com
- Share it on Facebook or Twitter

Appendix A: Questionnaire

Step 3: Questionnaire Form

Answer these questions for each person on your list to forgive. These reflective questions will help you gain a deeper understanding of your feelings concerning each person. There are additional forms in the appendix.

What was your relationship like prior to this event?

_____

_____

What did this person say or do to offend you?

_____

_____

How did it make you feel? (Try to be specific in identifying your feelings.)

_____

_____

_____

How has this offense negatively influenced your life?

_____

_____

Has the offense created an ongoing issue?

_____

_____

How has it impacted upon your relationship with yourself?

_____

_____

In what ways has it affected your relationship with others?

_____

_____

What is your relationship with that person like now?

_____

_____

Do you feel that you must receive an apology before you can forgive? _____

Additional thoughts and feelings concerning this individual.

_____

_____

Step 3: Questionnaire Form

What was your relationship like prior to this event?

_____

_____

What did this person say or do?

_____

_____

How did it make you feel? (Try to be specific in identifying your feelings.)

_____

_____

How has this person's wrongdoing negatively influenced your life?

_____

_____

Has the offense created an ongoing effect?

_____

_____

_____

_____

How has it impacted upon your relationship with yourself?

_____

_____

In what ways has it affected your relationship with others?

_____

_____

_____

What is your relationship with that person like now?

_____

_____

_____

Do you feel that you must receive an apology before you can forgive? _____

Additional thoughts and feelings concerning this individual.

_____

_____

_____

_____

APPENDIX B: BIBLIOGRAPHY

Amen, Daniel (2008). *Healing the Hardware of the Soul*. New York: Free Press.

Boerma, C. (2007). Physiology of anger. Retrieved from http://healthmad.com/mental-health/physiology-of-anger

Emoto, Masaru (2001). *The Hidden Messages in Water*. New York: Atria Books.

Emoto, Masaru (2003). *The True Power in Water*. New York: Atria Books.

Enright, R.D. & Fitzgibbons, R. (2015). *Forgiveness Therapy*. Washington, DC: APA Books.

Enright, R.D. https://internationalforgiveness.com/research.htm

Frankl, Viktor. (1959). *Man's Search for Meaning*. NY: Washington Square Press.

Frankl, Victor. (1988). *The Will to Meaning: Foundations and Applications of Logotherapy*. NY: Penguin Books.

Greer, S. & Morris, T. (1975). Psychological attributes of women who develop breast cancer: A controlled study. Journal of Psychosomatic Research, 19, 147-153.

Hendlin, Steven. (2004). *Overcoming the Inheritance Taboo. How to Preserve Relationships and Transfer Possessions*. NY: Penguin Books.

Hendricks, L., Bore, S., , Aslinia,D., & Morriss, G. (2013). The effects of anger on the brain and body. National Forum Journal of Counseling and Addiction, 2, 1-12.

Martinez-Lewi, Linda. (2008) *Freeing Yourself from the Narcissist in your Life*. NY: Penguin Books.

Pattakos, Alex. (2004). *Prisoners of Our Thoughts: Viktor Frankl's Principles for Discovering Meaning in Life and Work*. San Francisco, CA. Barrett-Koehler Publishers.

Pettingale, K.W., Greer, S., & Tee, D.E. (1977). Serum IgA and emotional expression in breast cancer patients. Psychosomatic Research, 21, 395-399.

Rosenfeld, Michael J. (2014). Couple Longevity in the Era of Same-Sex Marriage in the U.S. Journal of Marriage and Family, 76: 905-918.

Sood, Amit (2015). *The Mayo Clinic Handbook for Happiness: A Four-Step Plan for Resilient Living.* Boston, Mass. DaCapo Lifelong Books.

Thomas, S.P., Groer, M., Davis, M., Droppleman, P., Mozingo,J., & Pierce M. (2000), Anger and cancer: an analysis of the linkages. Cancer Nursing, 23, 344-349.

White, V.M., English, D.R., Coates, H., Lagerlund, M., Borland, R., et al. (2007). Is cancer risk associated with anger control and negative affect? Findings from a prospective cohort study. Psychosomatic Medicine, 69, 667-674.

Williamson, Marianne. (1996). *A Return to Love: Reflections on the Principles of "A Course in Miracles".* NY: HarperCollins Publishers.

About the Author

Nella Coiro is an author, a public speaker, a coach, workbook facilitator, and an online instructor. She holds both undergraduate and graduate degrees, and is a trained and experienced counselor. More recently, she has been certified as a life coach and a mindfulness practitioner. Nella is also an accomplished musician, and has performed professionally with her spouse in the past.

On a more personal level, she has overcome many challenges in her own life, and her work is focused upon helping others to do so, as well. Nella has been writing since her teenage years, and her articles and poetry can be found in many publications including Studio East Magazine and Supervision Journal.

In her free time, you might find her strumming her guitar, reading a good book, bowling, or catching a good movie. Nella was born and raised in the city, and now lives in Putnam County with her husband, Kenny, and their two hounds, Penelope and Alex.

Nella also accepts motivated clients for private forgiveness coaching work.

To learn more about Nella and her work, visit:
NellaCoiro.com

OTHER TITLES:

The Forgiveness Journey: Transcend Your Hurt, Transform Your Life

ISBN: 978-1-7339522-0-0 (paperback)

ISBN: 978-1-7339522-1-7 (ebook)

Audiobook: Narrated by SOVAS Voice Arts Award Winner Margo Trueblood.

COMING IN 2020

Discover Your Inner Warrior

www.ingramcontent.com/pod-product-compliance
Lightning Source LLC
Chambersburg PA
CBHW051352070526
44584CB00025B/3734